Costa
D

Emma Medara

*A Rock Climbing Guidebook
to the Sierra de Prades
and Surrounding Area*

Text and topos by Mark Glaister and Emma Medara
Computer artwork, design and layout by Alan James
Original ROCKFAX design
Ben Walker, Mick Ryan and Alan James
Printed by Clearpoint Colourprint, Nottingham
Distributed by Cordee (Tel: (+int) 44 (0) 116 254 3579)

Published by ROCKFAX Ltd. December 2002
© ROCKFAX Ltd. 2002, 1998
A CIP catalogue record is available from the British Library
ISBN 1 873341 55 5

ROCKFAX
Sheffield, UK and Bishop, CA, USA
Email UK: alan@rockfax.co.uk
Email USA: mick@rockfax.com

RRP £15.95 ($25, € 25.50)

ROCK FAX
rockfax.com

Cover: Pete O'Donovan (POD) on *Kiki (7b+)* La Mussara / *Pròtz 50* Photo: Angels Rius

ROCKFAX

PEAK GRITSTONE EAST (2001) - rockfax.com/peak_gritstone
The most popular UK guidebook ever covering the magnificent eastern gritstone edges of the Peak District. Full colour throughout, 288 pages, nearly 2000 routes and 50 action photos.
"..this book is as close to perfect a guidebook as we are likely to get."
- Ed Douglas, Climber Mag, February 2002
"It's a breath of fresh air. It's a revolution. Never has a guide book been so inspiring. You can now look at a crag that you have never been to and take a fairly educated guess as to whether you will enjoy the style of climbing it has to offer."
- Matt Heason, Planetfear.com, December 2001

COAST BLANCA, MALLORCA, EL CHORRO (2001) - rockfax.com/spain
Third edition of the most popular ROCKFAX guidebook to three brilliant climbing areas in Spain. Sport and some trad climbing. Now with 360 pages and nearly 3000 routes.
"This easily lives up to the very high standards that we have been accustomed to from the ROCKFAX range over the past eleven years" - Ben Heason, Planetfear.com, May 2001

YORKSHIRE GRITSTONE BOULDERING (2000) -
rockfax.com/yorkshire_bouldering
All the bouldering on the brilliant gritstone outcrops of Yorkshire, England.
320 pages, nearly 3500 problems over 17+ locations.
"..one day all guidebooks will look like this" - Simon Panton, Climber Mag, February 2001

DORSET (2000) - rockfax.com/dorset
Sport climbing, trad climbing, deep water soloing and bouldering on the south coast of England. 1500 routes on 272 pages including 32 pages of colour.
"Mighty fine; a job well done" - Mike Robertson, OTE, May 2000

PEAK BOULDERING (1998 and 2000) - rockfax.com/peak_bouldering
Gritstone bouldering in the Peak District, near Sheffield, England. The only guidebook available. 2nd Edition - 224 pages, 38 locations and 1600+ separate problems.
"Having had a chance to use the guide for myself, plus liaising with others, it has become apparent that it is pretty damn good." - Neil Bentley, High, August 1998

NORTH WALES LIMESTONE and NORTH WALES BOULDERING (1997)
rockfax.com/north_wales_limestone
Sport and traditional climbing found on the spectacular Ormes of Llandudno. Also includes a bouldering guide to North Wales. 224 pages, 800+ routes, 34 separate crags.

ISLANDS IN THE SKY - VEGAS LIMESTONE (2001) - rockfax.com/vegas
A guidebook to the rock climbing on Las Vegas and Great basin limestone in the USA.
224 pages, 652 routes.

RIFLE - BITE THE BULLET (1997)
Sport climbing on the limestone of Rifle Mountain Park in Colorado. 72 pages, 200+ routes.

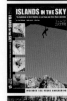

PEMBROKE (1995)
Traditional climbing on the Pembrokeshire Coast of South Wales. All the important routes are included. 112 pages, 450+ routes.

BISHOP BOULDERING SURVIVAL KIT (1999)
All the information you need for bouldering around Bishop in California.

CONTENTS

INTRODUCTION

Emma Medara pulling into the groove of *Obiang* (7b), Sector la Proa, La Mussara, *Page 43*. Photo: Highroglyphics.

The Costa Daurada is Catalunya's gold coast and is home not only to a kind winter climate but also to a wealth of superb sport climbing located in a dramatic and diverse setting. The climbing experience is second to none and many of the areas covered in this guide are as good as you can find anywhere for the travelling climber, whether it be days of mileage on grade 5s and 6s, or high quality 7s and 8s.

A variety of accommodation is available close to the climbing, ranging from apartments, villas and campsites down on the coast to more rural venues up in the hills, away from the beaches. If you have enjoyed the holiday climbing atmosphere on the Costa Blanca you will be in for an equally good time on the Costa Daurada. The weather during the autumn, winter and spring seasons is usually good for climbing and the vast majority of the crags have a sunny southerly aspect. The altitude of many crags is from 500m to 1000m, which means that air temperatures are cooler than on the coast but when the sun is out (which is most of the time) then it is warm. The altitude also means that climbing is a comfortable experience in the early autumn or late spring.

THE GUIDEBOOK

Although this guidebook contains nearly 1000 routes it is most definitely a *selected guidebook*. We have tried to provide a balanced selection which will guide the user to the best crags in each area covered. There are many more crags but a good number of them are of local interest only or do not provide significant numbers of good routes. We have personally visited all the crags and have not included those which we have felt to be of only limited appeal. As examples - we have not included the majority of routes on Crag Isabel at La Mussara because they are rather chossy and line-less, neither have we included the large crags of El Dard and its near neighbours in the Arbolí area as they are not quite as good as they appear on the topos and have a grade range already well catered for in the area (see El Falco). Other omissions are some major sectors where access is sensitive.

Pete O'Donovan (POD) on
irecta Reus (6b+) at La Riba, *Page 147*
hoto: Angels Rius

Craig Smith on the fine arete of *Esperó* (6b+) on Can Simiro, Arbolí. *Page 88.* Photo: Alan James.

HISTORY

Modern sport climbing was fully embraced throughout the region during the mid-eighties with the initial forays being a little faltering. Some relics of this period have very sportingly placed bolts and a plethora of chipped holds. As the scene has matured the numbers of routes, crags and participants have steadily grown, and several of the crags are now worked out. Of course, being Spain, unclimbed rock is not in short supply and much new development is in progress. This is especially evident on the huge ridge of Montsant; a crag with as much unclimbed rock as total rock on every other crag in this book added together.

OTHER GUIDEBOOKS

There are several more complete guidebooks now available to the area. All of these are available locally in the Tabac shops, the camp sites or online from **www.desnivel.es** (site in Spanish).

Montserrat (2001) - Luis Alfonso and Xavier Buxo
A fine guidebook to this area which was briefly mentioned in the first edition of Costa Daurada. Good topos covering all of the routes.

Mussara and Mont-ral (2001) - Luis Alfonso and Xavier Buxo
All the routes in these two major areas. An excellent addition for any climber who has made several visits to these areas and wishes to explore them more. Covers all the routes at Isabel, the far left-hand end of the TV Crags and several smaller sectors near the Mussara refuge. It also has information on Maset de Paisan at Mont-ral.

Arbolí (2002) - Luis Alfonso and Xavier Buxo
All the routes at Arbolí and El Falco. More sectors at the Roadside Crags plus information on other local crags like El Dard.

There is also a small topo available to cover Vilanova de Prades.

Steve Dunning below the crux of
La loca más loca del bodevil (7b+)
Sector Ca La Boja at Siurana. *Page 117.*
Photo: Pete Chadwick

Mark Glaister climbing *Yin-yang* (7b+) Sector Dels Ploms, Vilanova de Prades. *Page 139.* Photo: Highroglyphics

ACCESS and BEHAVIOUR

All the areas covered in the guide have good access from well-used, or designated, parking areas but please use common sense if problems of car parking congestion occur.
 - There are only two restrictions on climbing due to birds. **DO NOT CLIMB AT MOLA ROQUEROLA DURING THE BAN (1st Jan to 1st July).** Also there is a year-round ban on the right-hand side of Sector Can Marges Upper at Siurana.
- Outdoor fires are banned throughout the region.
- Please do not leave litter. This is a problem at the popular sectors, predominantly at weekends, when the crags become crowded.
- Sadly there is plenty of human faeces near the main crags. Try to go before you start the days cragging, but if you do feel the need, walk a good way from the crag and water supply and bury your waste at least 15cm deep.

FEEDBACK - THE COSTA DAURADA ROUTE DATABASE

www.rockfax.com/spain/database/

This database contains a listing of every route in the book with the possibility for you to lodge comments and vote on grades and star ratings. This information is essential to help us ensure complete and up-to-date coverage for all the climbs. We can then produce updates and make sure we get it right in subsequent editions. To make this system work we need the help of everyone who climbs in the Costa Daurada. We can not reflect opinions if we have not got them so if you think you have found a big sandbag of a route, or discovered a hidden gem that we have only given a single star to, let us know about it. We also want to know your general comments on all other aspects of this book. Use the forms at **www.rockfax.com/feedback/**

Rock Climbing Holidays and
Private Guiding throughout
Spain and beyond

Area Information Service

Preparation Courses

INFORMATION

Roofs of Morera de Montsant. Photo: Chris Craggs

Before you can start climbing you need to get to the area and sort out somewhere to stay. The following section may give you some pointers. More extensive and up-to-date information is available from the ROCKFAX web site on **www.rockfax.com**.

FLIGHTS
Reus has a seasonal airport (open from 1st May to 31st October) which is extremely close to the climbing areas. The flights to Reus are all charters which can vary dramatically in price depending on the school holidays. Information on charter flights is available from travel agents, newspapers and the following web sites: **www.air-travel.co.uk** - **www.cheap-flights-reus.com**
www.flightsavers.co.uk - **www.cheapflights.com** - **www.charterflights.co.uk**
Barcelona is the next nearest airport which is open all year round. **EasyJet** (www.easyjet.com) fly there from Stansted, Liverpool, Amsterdam, Bristol and East Midlands.**BMIBaby** (**www.bmibaby.com**) fly to Barcelona from East Midlands, Cardiff, Edinburgh and Glasgow. **Virgin** (**www.virginexpress.com**) fly to Barcelona from Brussels and have good prices connecting through Brussels from a number of destinations including London, Stockholm and Gothenburg. The long and arduous drive through France may will only be an option for those with a lot of time, or on a long climbing trip. The most relaxing journey, but the most expensive, is the 'cruise' from Portsmouth to Bilbao (P&O) or Plymouth to Santander (Brittany). From the Spanish ports, it takes about 5 hours to drive to the Costa Daurada.

CAR HIRE
Although the Costa Daurada is a good area to go if you are on a limited budget and don't want to hire a car, having your own transport is definitely preferable. Car hire is best arranged from the UK and the cost for the standard little car ranges from £80-£150 per week. There are hire car companies at the airports but their prices high.
www.europcar.com - **www.premiercarhire.co.uk** - **www.hertz.co.uk** - **www.easycar.com**

There is some car crime in the area, be particularly careful at La Mussara, Siurana and La Riba. Don't leave any valuables or other objects visible in the car.

INFORMATION

GETTING AROUND

Many of the roads within the mountains are slow and windy and choosing the quickest route from *A to B* is not always simple. The climb up into the mountains tends to be very slow; once there the roads are a bit less tortuous. If you are staying on the coast, allow at least an hour to get to the main areas. If you are intending to visit Mont-ral, La Riba or Cogullons then use the C14 towards Alcover. Vilanova de Prades can take a while to reach from everywhere unless you are camped underneath it.

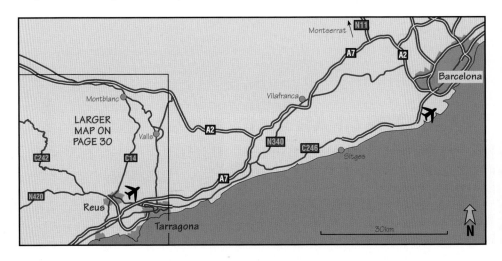

Getting on the right road from Reus Airport - From the airport, drive into Reus to reach the ring road ('Rondes'). If you are heading for the northern areas, turn off the ring road onto the C14 signed to 'Montblanc'. (**NOTE -** there is a large *Carrefour* supermarket just beyond this junction). If you intend to stay at Mussara, Arbolí or Siurana, continue around the ring road to locate the N420 sign posted to 'Falset', then pick up the appropriate road into the mountains from the map opposite.

Getting there from Barcelona Airport - From the airport head towards Barcelona but quickly turn north onto the A2. Follow this onto the A7 and head west in the direction of 'Tarragona' and 'Valencia'. For the northern crags branch right after Vilafranca on the A2 signed to 'Lleida'. Montblanc is exit 9. For Mussara, Arbolí or Siurana, stay on the A7 to junction 34. Then head into Reus past the airport, to the ring road. Drive around the ring road to locate the N420 sign posted to 'Falset'.

WITHOUT A CAR

There are a number of crags with camping, or refuges, located close by, which should give enough climbing for a week. Check the accommodation information on page 16 for a list of likely bases.

Trains service the area with stations at Reus, La Riba and Montblanc. A bus service operates locally with stops at Barcelona, Tarragona, Salou, Cambrils, Cornudella and Prades. There is a bus out of Cornudella in early morning which returns from Barcelona mid afternoon.

INFORMATION

WHEN TO GO
The optimum times to visit are October through to May. The winter months can have periods of cold and wet weather but then it can also be wonderfully sunny and settled. The summer months, June through to the end of September, are very hot but, if you can confine your climbing activities to the morning and evening, you will have no problem getting routes ticked. From November to the end of April, you will have to fly to Barcelona or Gerona.

	Jan	Feb	Mar	Apr	May	Jun	Jul	Aug	Sep	Oct	Nov	Dec

TRAVEL INSURANCE
You are strongly advised to take out travel insurance before your trip. If you are in any doubt, just ask someone who has had cause to used it!
Foundry Travel Insurance - Web: **www.foundrytravel.com** Tel: 0114 2755806
BMC Travel Insurance - Web: **www.thebmc.com** Tel: 0161 445 4747

SHOPS
Cornudella and Prades have small shops for day-to-day provisions. There are supermarkets at Vals and Montblanc and it is a good idea to stock up at one of these before heading into the mountains. There is a huge *Carrefour* hyper-market in Reus (near the C14 'Montblanc' turning, off the ring road) and another big supermarket in Tarragona.
Most fo the shops in the small villages will be closed in the middle of the day.

CLIMBING SHOPS
There are two dedictaed climbing shops in the region and one other shop of interest:
K2 - centre of Tarragona. Address - Cos del Bou, 12, 43003 Tarragona. Tel. 977 23 86 30.
Uka Uka - 4 Alcalder Costa (off Avda de Catalunya), Lleida. (Near Tourist Information).
No Limits - This large sports store is situated at Selva del Camp on the C14 between Alcover and Reus. This stocks a limited selection of climbing gear.

TOURIST OFFICES - Check www.costadaurada.org
MONTBLANC, OFICINA COMARCAL DE TURISME
Antiga Església St. Francesc. 43400 MONTBLANC. Tel: 977 861 733 Fax: 977 861 733

CAPAFONTS, OFICINA MUNICIPAL DE TURISME
Les Foints, 7. 43364 CAPAFONTS. Tel: 977 868 049 Fax: 977 868 049

CORNUDELLA DE MONTSANT, PATRONAT MUNICIPAL DE TURISME
Carrer Comte de Rius, 10. 43360 CORNUDELLA DE MONTSANT
Tel: 977 821 000 Fax: 977 821 000
www.cornudella.altanet.org Email: **tur.cornudella@altanet.org**

PRADES, OFICINA MUNICIPAL DE TURISME
Plaça Major, 2. 43364 PRADES. Tel: 977 868 302 Fax: 977 868 197
www.pradesmontsant.com

ULLDEMOLINS, PATRONAT DE CULTURA I TURISME
Carrer Saltadora, 26. 43363 ULLDEMOLINS. Tel. 977 561 578 Fax 977 561 583
www.fut.es/~ajtullde Email:**ajtullde@tinet.fut.es**

*All phone numbers are **+34 drop the 9** from outside Spain.*

ACCOMMODATION

APARTMENTS

Along the Costa Daurada there are possibilities for renting apartments although these are harder to come by in the winter months. You may be able to arrange package-type holiday deals with your travel agent. Alternatively, if you search through the travel sections of newspapers, you will be able to find telephone numbers to arrange such accommodation yourself. The two main destinations for holidaying Brits are Salou and Cambrils. The following web sites have sophisticated search routines for finding accommodation - **www.costadaurada.org** (English) **www.tourspain.es** (English) and **www.publintur.es** (Spanish).

Other possibilities are *Casa Pages* - rural accommodation situated in the Prades region. You will be able to get information on these from one of the tourist offices listed on the previous page.

Also check **www.rockfax.com/costa_daurada/accom.html**

FONDA CAL BLASI

Situated in the historical centre of Montblanc, Fonda Cal Blasi is a delightful guest house constructed from a 12th century building. The antique structure of the building has been preserved whilst the Catalunyan concept of a "fonda" (a small family hotel serving home-made food) has been updated to give maximum comfort for our guests.

Fonda Cal Blasi, c\ Alenyà 11, 43400 Montblanc , Tarragona
Tel: +34 (9)77 861 336 Fax: +34 (9)77 86 29 31
Email: carlescarme@fondacalblasi.com (English possible)
Web site: www.fondacalblasi.com

REFUGES

You could quite happily base yourself at any one of the refuges in the Sierra de Prades. Each one is different in character and offers different facilities. It is a good way to meet other climbers and each refuge holds a route book. If you are planning to stay at a refuge you will need to bring all your own equipment including stoves, plates, cutlery and sleeping bags.

La Mussara

Set in a lovely surrounding with great views down to the coast 1000m below. You can either camp here, which includes use of the refuge facilities, or you can sleep in the refuge. You can buy meals, beer, drinks and sometimes chalk. The refuge guardians speak a little English. It can get busy at the weekends with people from the cities.

APPROACH - see map on page 34

Mont-ral

Situated in the small village of Mont-ral, this refuge is more like a hostel. It has room and dormitory-type accommodation. The guardians provide meals, drinks and beer. There is a telephone at the refuge.

APPROACH - see map on page 70

Arbolí

Based in the village of Arbolí, this refuge is very basic. There are no camping facilities just dormitory-type accommodation.

APPROACH - see map on page 82

- Meals available
- Good water close by
- Shops close by
- Crags you can walk to
- Showers

ACCOMMODATION

Siurana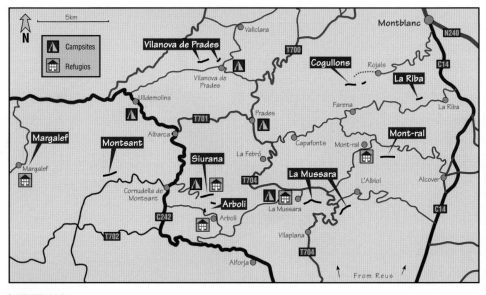

This refuge has its own atmosphere and scene. Dormitory accommodation is available along with meals and drinks. A party-piece bouldering wall hangs above the eating tables, perfect when you've had a few beers. *Photo page 96.*
APPROACH - see map on page 106

The refuge at Cogullons has now closed although free camping is still possible. There is also a refuge in the village of Margalef although it is only open at very busy times.

- Meals available
- Good water close by
- Shops close by
- Crags you can walk to
- Showers

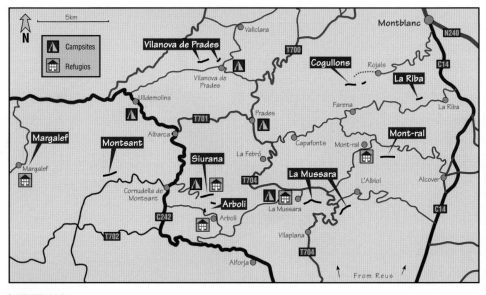

CAMPING

There are numerous campsites to be found in both the Prades and Montsant region, as well as along the coast. These provide a real alternative to renting an apartment and are open all year round. Many of the sites are full-facility sites with everything from swimming pools to restaurants. Being based at one of the sites listed below will mean that you are conveniently located for the climbing.

Camping Prades - Prades

A full-facility site situated in the small town of Prades which is smack bang in the centre of the climbing. The site is a popular weekend retreat for the city folk of Tarragona and Reus and can get very busy. Facilities include hot showers, washing machines, shop, telephones, restaurant/bar. There are also some bungalows for rent. The town of Prades contains a bakery, grocery, shops, bars, restaurants, bank etc. all within walking distance of the campsite. It is worth being aware that Prades is at an altitude of about 1000m and, because of its location right in the centre of the Prades mountains, it does tend to catch cold and damp weather in the winter months, but you can soon drive out of this on your way to one of the climbing areas.

    APPROACH - Prades is central to the area and the campsite is well signed.

ACCOMMODATION

Camping La Ruta del Cister -Vilanova de Prades

Not to be confused with the town of Prades, Vilanova de Prades is a small village 8km from Prades. It is well situated for all the climbing areas especially Vilanova de Prades. You can almost stumble out of your tent and be on the crag. As well as camping, this full-facility site also has small chalet/bungalows for rent which can accommodate up to 8 people. Again the site has all facilities such as hot showers, washing machines, games room, bar, shop, play area. A route book of the Vilanova de Prades climbing is kept in the bar.
Tel/Fax: +34 (9)77 86 90 50 **www.svt.es/serraprades**. E-mail: **serraprades@svt.es**
APPROACH - see map on page 131

Camping Montsant Park - Ulldemolins

Another good site situated between Cornudella and Vilanova de Prades on the C242, near to the town of Ulldemolins. Tel: +34 (9)77 56 17 08
APPROACH - The campsite is situated just south of the town of Ulldemolins. See map on previous page.

- Meals available

- Good water close by

- Shops close by

- Crags you can walk to

- Showers

La Mussara Refuge

There are some very nice camping spots amongst the pine trees surrounding the Mussara refuge and you can use all the facilities of the refuge (bring your own stove etc) or you can buy meals and beer from the guardians.
APPROACH - see map on page 35

Siurana

There is a new campsite at Siurana located 200 metres before the large parking area before the village. Run by Toni Arbones, it has good showers and washrooms. There may now be some apartments for the winter. There is also a clubhouse that serves drinks and food. Topos and new route information are held there and Toni sells 5.10 climbing shoes and chalk.
Camping Siurana, Coll de Ginebre, 43362 Siurana, Tarragona.
APPROACH - see map on page 98

Siurana Village. Photo: Highroglyphics

The Coast

There are campsites along the coast which are not as conveniently located for the climbing, but are well situated if you will be spending some time enjoying the beach. It is much warmer on the coast in the winter months and many of the sites are open throughout the 'off season' months.

FREE CAMPING

There are several possibilities for free camping for those on a tight budget. As usual you will have to sacrifice certain things like easily available water, proper toilets and security for your belongings, but you will be able to get close to the climbing and usually be in a very beautiful situation. If you are camping for free somewhere it is possible to pay for a shower at the Prades campsite. The popular sites are on the approach to La Riba and up the Cogullons under the old refuge (no problem with security there).

CLIMBING INFORMATION

GEAR

For all of the sport routes in this guide 16 quickdraws and a 60m single rope are adequate. At El Falco a couple more quickdraws may be needed on some of the really long pitches if you intend to leave any in the lower-off chain. A number of sectors have routes that are considerably longer than 30m and consequently an intermediate lower-off will be necessary. Those people with 50m and 55m single ropes will need to exercise much caution in all areas as many pitches are over 27m in length. **ALWAYS TIE A KNOT IN THE ROPE BEFORE LOWERING.** If you are intending to tackle any of the routes which require gear a full rack of cams and nuts will be necessary.

TOPOS AND SYMBOLS

The idea behind all the various features of a ROCKFAX guidebook is to help you find and assess the most appropriate climbing quickly and accurately. To help there are many maps, symbols, tables and descriptions, all of which are relatively simple to follow and need little explanation. If you do not like reading long-winded descriptions, or English is not your first language, then you should still be able to use the guide. Conversely, if you hate maps and your brain cannot cope with 2-dimensional representations of a 3-dimensional world, there are always the text approaches and route descriptions to fall back on.

GRADES

In general the grades are pretty friendly and consistently applied, in common with most other popular Spanish areas. Many of the routes in this guide are long sustained affairs so the grades are often a reflection of accumulated difficulty, rather than short bouldery or cruxy experiences. If you are fit then you may even find a few soft touches. Some of the older routes have recently been pushed up a notch by consensus having become a little polished or blatantly under-graded in the past.

BRITISH TRAD GRADE / Sport Grade / UIAA / USA / Australian

British Trad Grades (diamond symbols, top to bottom): Mod (Moderate), Diff (Difficult), VDiff (Very Difficult), HVD (Hard Very Difficult), Sev (Severe), HS (Hard Severe) 4a, VS (Very Severe) 4c, HVS (Hard Very Severe) 4c/5b, E1 5a/5c, E2 5b, E3 5c/6a, E4 6a, E5 6a/6c, E6 6b/6c, E7 6c/7a, E8 6c/7a, E9 7a/7b, E10 7a/7b.

Sport Grade	UIAA	USA	Australian
1	I	5.1	4
2	II	5.2	6
2+	III	5.3	
3-	III+	5.4	8
3	IV	5.5	10
	IV+		
3+	V-	5.6	12
4	V	5.7	14
4+	V+	5.8	
5	VI-	5.9	16
5+	VI	5.10a	18
6a	VI+	5.10b	19
6a+	VII-	5.10c	20
6b	VII	5.10d	
6b+	VII+	5.11a	21
6c	VIII-	5.11b	22
6c+	VIII-	5.11c	23
7a	VIII	5.11d	
7a+	VIII+	5.12a	24
7b	IX-	5.12b	25
7b+	IX-	5.12c	26
7c	IX	5.12d	27
7c+	IX+	5.13a	28
8a	X-	5.13b	29
8a+	X	5.13c	30
8b	X	5.13d	31
8b+	X+	5.14a	32
8c	XI-	5.14b	33
8c+	XI	5.14c	34
9a	XI	5.14d	35
9a+	XI+	5.15a	36

COLOUR CODING

The routes are colour-coded corresponding to a grade band.

GREEN SPOTS - Everything at grade 4+ and under. Mostly these should be good for beginners and those wanting an easy life.

ORANGE SPOTS - 5 to 6a+ inclusive. General ticking routes for those with more experience.

RED SPOTS - 6b to 7a inclusive. Routes for the very experienced and keen climber. Climbers operating in this grade band are bound to have a good time in the Costa Daurada.

BLACK SPOTS - 7a+ and above. The hard stuff is spread liberally across the Daurada crags. All unknown lines are also given black spots although they might not be that hard.

CLIMBING INFORMATION

Route Symbols

 A good route

 A very good route

 A brilliant route

A poor route.
A bag of......!

 Technical climbing involving complex or trick moves

 Powerful moves requiring big arms

Sustained climbing, either long and pumpy or with lots of hard moves

Fingery climbing - sharp holds!

 A route which needs wires and friends.

 Fluttery climbing with big fall potential

 A long reach is helpful/essential

Area Symbols

 Approach
Approach walk time, and angle.

 Buttress can be reached on foot from a campsite or refugio.

 Sunshine
Approximate time when the sun is on the crag.

 Access Restriction
With time when climbing is not allowed.

 Lower-offs on most routes

 Some multi-pitch routes

A buttress with dry climbing in the rain

 Slabby climbing

 Vertical wall climbing

 Steep climbing

Topos

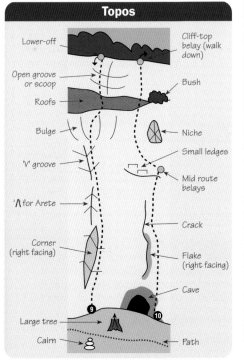

Lower-off

Cliff-top belay (walk down)

Open groove or scoop

Roofs

Bush

Bulge

Niche

'V' groove

Small ledges

Mid route belays

'Λ for Arete

Crack

Corner (right facing)

Flake (right facing)

Cave

Large tree

Cairn

Path

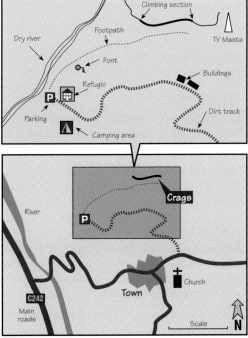

Climbing section

Dry river

Footpath

TV Masts

Font

Buildings

Refugio

Parking

Dirt track

Camping area

Crags

River

Church

Town

C242

Main roads

Scale

N

La Costa Daurada
...probablement la meilleure grimpe en Espagne!

La bande côtière est, à n'en pas douter, un paradis touristique largement développé, lorsque dans les terres se trouve la chaîne de montagnes calcaires du nom de la Sierra de Prades. Celle-ci est une zone d'escalade relativement connue depuis de nombreuses années, avec des falaises telles que La Riba et Siurana. Plus récemment, les vastes possibilités de la Sierra de Prades et les vastes étendues de falaises aux alentours ont été développées, mais non documentées. Ces lieux comprennent de superbes parois telles que

Falco avec ses voies d'endurance de 45 mètres de hauteur, ou bien les piliers sensationnels de Montsant. La richesse en voies simples ou en relais doubles de ces falaises est égalée par d'autres regions d'Espagne, mais la concentration en voies de qualité y est sans contexte plus élevée que partout ailleurs.

LE GUIDE

Ce livre contient toute l'information requise concernant toutes les voies et falaises principales de la region. C'est aussi le seul guide à jour disponible. Toute l'information est illustrée avec cartes, topos et symboles, donc même si vous ne parlez pas bien l'anglais, vous ne devriez pas avoir de problèmes à accéder aux lieux et à les évaluer.

EQUIPEMENT

La plupart de l'escalade décrite dans ce livre est sur parois totalement equipées. Certaines voies nécessitent un petit jeu de coinceurs; elles sont indiquées par le symbole ![symbole]. .

INFORMATION SUPPLÉMENTAIRE

Tous les guides de la série ROCKFAX sont complétés par un site Internet à **www.rockfax.com**.

ROCKFAX

ROCKFAX consiste d'Alan James au Royaume-Uni et de Mick Ryan aux États-Unis. Ça fait depuis 1990 que nous faisons des guides d'escalade sur des endroits situées dans le monde entier. Vous trouverez des renseignements sur toutes nos publications sur notre website **www.rockfax.com**

Email (Royaume-Uni): **alan@rockfax.co.uk**

Email (États-Unis): **mick@rockfax.com**

Symboles

 Bonne voie

 Escalade technique nécessitant des mouvements complexes et astucieux.

 Voie nécessitant quelques coinceurs.

 Très bonne voie

 Requiert des bras solides pour des mouvements de forces.

 Escalade angoissante avec possibilité de grandes chutes

 Voie Majeure

 Escalade de continuité, longue et avec bouteilles garanties ou bien avec beaucoup de mouvements durs

 Les grands seront avantagés.

 Une voie médiocre. De la m.......!

Escalade à doigts – prises coupantes!

Symboles de Parois

 Approche - Temps de marche d'approche et pente.

Falaise accessible à pied depuis un camping ou un refuge

Soleil - Heures approximatives auxquelles la paroi est exposée au soleil.

Restrictions sur les Parois
Lorsque ce symbole apparaît sur le topo, il existe une restriction concernant l'escalade sur cette falaise.

 Moulinettes sur la plupart des voies

 Dalle

 Plusieurs longueurs

 Vertical

 Protégé de la pluie

 Surplomb

Topos

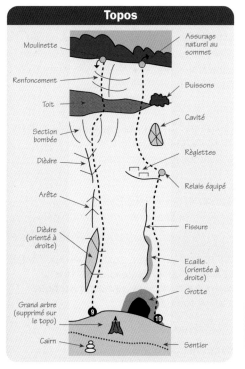

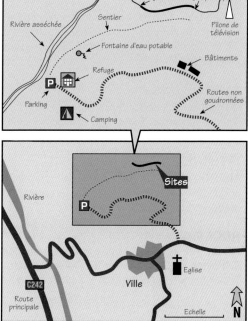

Die Costa Daurada
...wahrscheinlich das beste Klettergebiet in Spanien!

Das Klettergebiet der Costa Daurada in Spanien liegt im Südwesten von Barcelona. Die Küste ist erwartungsgemäß ein gut erschlossenes Touristenparadies, aber nur wenig weiter im Inland findet man die Kalksteinformationen namens Sierra Prades. Schon seit Jahren ist dieses Klettergebiet hinreichend bekannt durch Felsen wie La Riba und Siurana. Erst kürzlich wurde das enorme Kletterpotential der Sierra de Prades und der sie umgebenden weiten

Felsformationen ausgebaut, bislang jedoch noch nicht dokumentiert. Dies schließt wunderbare Felsen wie Falco mit seinen 45m langen Kraftrouten oder den überwältigenden Pfeiler von Montsant ein. Die Fülle von Einseil- und Mehrseilrouten kommt denen im übrigen Spanien gleich, aber die Konzentration von Qualitätsrouten ist unbestreitbar höher als anderswo.

DER FÜHRER
Dieses Buch enthält jegliche Informationen, die für alle Hauptrouten und Felsen im Gebiet benötigt werden. Es ist überdies der einzige aktuelle Führer, der erhältlich ist. Alle Informationen sind durch Karten, Skizzen und Symbole illustriert, die es ermöglichen, auch ohne umfassende Englischkenntnisse die verschiedenen Gebiete zu erkunden.

AUSRÜSTUNG
Die meisten Kletterrouten in diesem Buch beschreiben Touren auf voll ausgerüsteten Sportkletterfelsen. Für einige Routen wird ein geringes Ausmaß an Ausrüstung benötigt. Diese Touren sind durch das Symbol 🪝 gekennzeichnet.

INTERNET
Alle ROCKFAX Führer werden in einer umfassenden Web Seite **www.rockfax.com** vorgestellt. Diese enthalten Erneuerungen, Feedback Formulare und umfassende generelle Kletterinformationen.

ROCKFAX
ROCKFAX sind Alan James in Großbritannien und Mick Ryan in Amerika. Seit 1990 schreiben wir Kletterführer für Gebiete in der ganzen Welt. Informationen zu unseren Publikationen befinden sich auf unserer Webseite **www.rockfax.com**

E-mail (UK): **alan@rockfax.co.uk**

E-mail (USA): **mick@rockfax.com**

Symbole

 Lohnende Kletterei

 sehr Lohnende Kletterei

 brilliante Kletterei

 Unschöne Kletterei. Besser etwas anderes unternehmen ...

 Technisch anspruchsvolle Tour mit trickreichen Zügen.

 Anstrengende Züge. Erfordert dicke Oberarme.

 Durchgehend anstrengende Tour; entweder anhaltend schwer oder mit einer Reihe harter Züge.

 Kleingriffige, rauhe Kletterei - nichts für zarte Hände.

 Kletterei, die Sicherung durch Klemmkeile u.ä. erfordert.

 Heikle Kletterei mit hohem Sturzpotential, aber nicht allzu gefährlich.

 Lange Arme sind hilfreich.

Felsymbole

 Zugang
Zeit und Steilheit des Zugangsweges.

 Der Fels ist zu Futs vom Camping oder Refugio aus innerhalb weniger minuten erreichbar.

 Sonnenschein
Zeit, zu der der Felsen in der Sonne liegt.

 Beschränkungen am Fels
Einschränkungen beim Klettern für den entsprechenden Fels.

 Umlenkungen existieren in den meisten Routen

 mehrere Seillängen

 Trockener Fels bei Regen

 Plattige Reibungsprobleme

 Hauptsächlich senkrechte Probleme

 Hauptsächlich steile Probleme

Topos

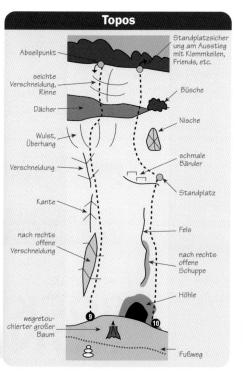

Karte

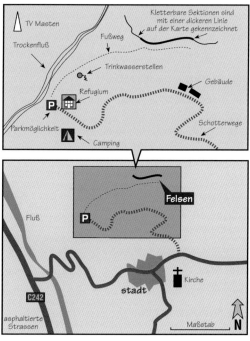

ADVERTISERS

ROCKFAX is very grateful to the following companies, shops and climbing walls, who have supported this guidebook.

AWESOME WALLS (Page 13) - Climbing wall
St. Alban's Church, Athol Street, Liverpool, L5 9XT. Tel: 0191 2303793
www.awesomewalls.co.uk

BENDCRETE (Page 47) - Climbing walls, holds, mats
Aqueduct Mill, Tame Street, Stalybridge, Cheshire, SK15 1ST.
Tel: 0161 3383046 Fax: 0161 338 7956 www.bendcrete.com

BMC INSURANCE (Page 11) - Travel insurance
Tel: 0161 445 4747 Fax: 0161 445 4500 www.thebmc.com

FONDA CAL BLASI (Page 16) - Guest house
c\ Alenyà 11, 43400 Montblanc , Tarragona
Tel: +34 (9) 77 86 13 36 Fax: +34 (9) 77 86 29 31
www.fondacalblasi.com

NEEDLESPORTS (Page 15) - Shop and online shop
56 Main Street, Keswick, Cumbria, CA12 5JS.
Tel: 017687 72227 Fax: 017687 75593 www.needlesports.com

OUTSIDE (Page 17) - Shops
Peak - Main Road, Hathersage, S32 1BB. Tel: 01433 651936
Snowdonia - The Old Baptist Chapel, Llanberis, LL55 4EN. Tel: 01286 871534
Calver - Baslow Road, Calver, S32 3XH. Tel: 01433 631111
www.outside.co.uk

PATRONAT DE TURISME DE LA DIPUTACIÓ (Outside back cover)
Tourist Information - www.costadaurada.org

ROCK + RUN (Page 11) - Shops and online shop
The Lakes - 3-4 Cheapside, Ambleside, LA22 0AB. Tel: 01539 433660
Mail Order - Tel: 015394 32855 www.rockrun.com

ROCK and SUN (Page 9) - Climbing holidays and private guiding
Rock and Sun, 66 Willsbridge Hill, Willsbridge, Bristol, BS30 6EU.
Tel: 07880 773 786 www.rockandsun.com

ROCKSPORT (Page 21) - Shop
at *The Edge* and 392 Psalter Lane, Banner Cross, Sheffield, S11 8UW.
Tel: 0114 266 7333 www.sheffieldclimbing.co.uk

ROCKWORKS (Inside back cover) - Climbing walls, holds, training aids.
Ouseburn Workshops, 36 Lime Street, Newcastle-upon-Tyne, NE1 2PN.
Tel: 0191 230 3793 www.rockworks.co.uk

SNOW & ROCK (Inside front cover) - Shops
Surrey Superstore - 99 Fordwater Road, Chertsey, KT16 8HH. Tel: 01932 566 886
Bristol Superstore - Shield Retail Centre, Bristol, BS34 7BQ. Tel: 0117 914 3000
Kensington - 188 Kensington High Street, London, W8 7RG. Tel: 0207 937 0872
Port Solent Superstore - The Boardwalk, Portsmouth, PO6 4TP. Tel: 02392 205 388
Holborn - 150 Holborn, Corner Gray's Inn Road, WC1X 8HG. Tel: 0207 831 6900
Covent Garden Superstore - 4 Mercer St., London WC2H 9QA. Tel: 02392 205 388
Birmingham - 14 Priory Queensway, Birmingham, B4 6BS. Tel: 0121 236 8280
www.snowandrock.com

THE EDGE CLIMBING CENTRE (Page 21) - Climbing wall
John Street, Sheffield, S2 4QU.
Tel: 0114 275 8899 Fax: 0114 273 8899 www.sheffieldclimbing.co.uk

THE FOUNDRY INSURANCE (Page 15) - Insurance
45 Mowbray Street, Sheffield. Tel: 0114 279 6331
www.foundrytravel.com

ACKNOWLEDGEMENTS

It has been quite an eye-opener writing this guidebook. There have been plenty of highlights and good times and there have also been some frustrating times. Living in the small confines of our van certainly has its moments, especially when opinions differ, one person's topo is better than the other, I think the route is powerful when Mark thinks it is a slab and one is having a better climbing day than the other. So after a year of working together in various states of harmony, and now seeing all our efforts in print, I would of course like to thank Mark for being a good mate, companion, climbing partner, scrabble partner (easy to beat!) and providing me with some ace laughs.

We have compiled the book by ourselves but several people we have met, or who have been to the area, have provided useful information, encouragement and some good companionship whiling away the long winter evening hours, drinking the local tipple and telling funny stories in our mobile home. These people are Chris Hertel, Robyn Embry, Rebekah Smith, Jon Bibby, Matt Jones, Gunn Johnsen, Bev Hull, Nigel Tuckley, Duncan McCallum. Several people have also been out to the area and come back with their comments and advice and they are Johnny and Stella Adams, John Earl and team, Ruth Ashton, Lynne Williams, Dave Marsh, Dave Hainsworth, Simon Webster, Simon Christy, James Goodman. And finally, thanks to Niff for giving us this opportunity and for producing such an excellent presentation of our work and showcase for our photography.

Finally, I would like to dedicate this guide book to my mother, whose amazing positive attitude surely must be an inspiration to my family and all those who know her.

Emma Williams (now Emma Medara) - October 1998

ROCKFAX Acknowledgments 2002
Remembering everyone who has helped with a guidebook is a difficult task at the best of times, never mind in the hectic pre-publishing rush which tends to be the moment that you write the Acknowledgements page. Occasionally some people get forgotten and in the last edition we forgot to mention one very important set of people; namely the local climbers who put all the work into equipping the routes. Without their efforts we would have nothing to climb and in this edition we would like to thank them not just for all the bolting and new routing, but also for maintaining the area and documenting the routes. Many of the local climbers run refuges or campsites, so just by visiting and staying in the area you are supporting them, however please also support the local guidebooks (page 6), respect the area and make use of the new route information kept in the refuges.

This stunning full-colour edition of the book has been enhanced with some superb action photography. A lot has come from the authors Mark and Emma, and I have re-used many shots from the last edition, however there have also been some great new contributions from Pete O'Donovan (POD) and Angels Rius, Chris Craggs and Pete Chadwick. POD and Angels have also put in a great effort reading through the text to check the Catalunyan spellings and add their extensive knowledge of the area to the book. Thanks are especially due to them and I wish I'd asked them last time! Since the last edition I have received loads of feedback by email and via the web site. A special mention to Nick Smith, Richard Hardicre, Jon Dunsdon and Ludek Kolesa for their extensive contributions. Also thanks to Simon Bingham, Neal Carroll, Rob Allen, Al Evans, Geraldine Taylor, Bridget Perkins and Jeremy, Richard Plant, Jeff Wincott, Sami Salonen, George Ridge, Janet Horrocks, M. Fortuny, P. Canut, F. Iranzo, Hilary Sharp and Jon deMontjoye for their feedback. I would like to thank my proof readers Paul Dearden, Mike James and Liz James and to Mick Ryan for the trans-atlantic support.

Mark Glaister has put in a big effort this time to help update the information but, of course, most of the really excellent work in the topos, descriptions, text and maps was already done in the last edition by himself and Emma; this time we have had the chance to enhance it all using full colour. Hopefully we have made an even better *presentation of your work and showcase for your photography*; it certainly deserves it.

Thanks also to Henriette, Hannah, Sam and Lydia.

Alan James - October 2002

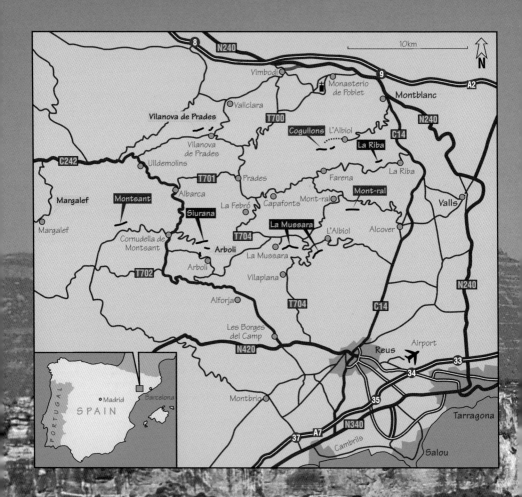

Costa
Daurada

Emma Medara climbing *Per tutatis* (7a+) El Falco, at Arbolí. *Page 95.* Photo: Highroglyphics

La Mussarra
Mont-ral
Arbolí
Siurana
Montsant
Vilanova de Prades
La Riba
Cogullons
Margalef

CRAG	No. of ROUTES	↓VS ↓4	VS 4	HVS 5	E1 6a	E2 6b	E3 6c	E4 7a	E5 7b	E6 7c	E7 8a	E8 8b
LA MUSSARA AREA	**258** TOTAL		7	40	57	47	35	31	28	10	3	
TV CRAGS	134		4	20	32	22	15	15	17	7	2	
LO RAVAL	13				2	2	2	3	2	1		
LO SOTERRANI	80		3	32	32	15	7	8	7	1	1	
ISABEL	13			1	2	4	5	1				
LES CAMPANILLES	18				1	4	6	4	1	1		
MONT-RAL	**62** TOTAL	1	6	9	16	12	10		3	5	1	
ARBOLI AREA	**86** TOTAL	1	5	11	8	8	14	16	16	3	4	
ARBOLI	59	1	5	11	7	6	7	11	9		2	
EL FALCO	27				1	2	7	5	7	3	2	
SIURANA AREA	**190** TOTAL			19	15	22	32	26	30	22	13	1
VALLEY CRAGS	50			2	1	8	6	7	6	8	7	5
VILLAGE CRAGS	140			18	13	14	26	19	24	14	6	6
MONTSANT	**36** TOTAL					5	8	3	3	7	1	
VILANOVA DE PRADES AREA	**138** TOTAL		11	21	19	13	18	15	16	13	6	6
CAMPING CRAGS	90		7	16	19	10	15	11	7	5		
OUT OF TOWN CRAGS	48		4	5		3	3	4	9	8	6	6
LA RIBA	**69** TOTAL		2	8	15	23	8	6	13	12	8	
LES COGULLONS	**97** TOTAL		3	15	23	10	6	16	13	11		
MOLA ROQUEROLA	51		5	12		4	4	8	10	8		
LES GRALLES	46		3	10	11	6	2	8	3	3		
MARGALEF	**81** TOTAL		11	20	18	16	16	7	7	5		

Approach walk	Sunshine or shade	Quality gear routes	Multi-pitch routes	Dry routes in the rain	Can walk to/from camping/refuge	Access	SUMMARY	Page
							Largest area in the book and a great place to start your trip. Plenty across the grade range. Need a car to get to most crags, can get very hot and can also get misty.	34
5 min to 10 min	Lots of sun	✓	✓				Many sectors with dozens of pitches from 5+ to 7a. Sectors Roure and Primitiu are popular 'first day' crags.	36
15 min	Lots of sun						Small sector which is best combined with Isabel Crag. A sun-trap so it is best visited on cool days.	52
15 min	Lots of sun	✓					The epitome of a holiday crag. Loads of routes, sun and stunning views over the Med.	56
20 min	Morning						Large broken and vegetated crag with one very good sector. Approach is awkward. Nice and cool in the afternoon.	64
40 min	Afternoon				✓		Excellent sustained wall pitches. A first class day out for the competent grade 6 team. A long approach trek.	66
10 min to 15 min	Afternoon		✓		✓		Good for parties with mixed abilities or those looking for long grade 6s. River for swimming and good picnicking potential except in Summer.	69
							The Arbolí crags are magnificently situated across the valley from the Siurana Village promontory. Much less busy but with some equally fine climbing.	80
5 min	Afternoon				✓		Very accessible and would make a good venue if time is short. A good mix of grades.	84
5 min	Afternoon				✓		A magnificent crag. Huge pitches in a beautiful setting overlooking Siurana and the Montsant range.	91
							Siurana launched hard climbing in the area. Much-visited by climbers from all over the world. Far easier to get up to now that the approach road has been upgraded (as have some of the routes!).	96
2 min to 10 min	Lots of sun			✓	✓		Stunning orange and grey streaked walls with tufa pillars. Mainly harder grades. Dry in the rain.	99
1 min to 15 min	Lots of sun			✓	✓		Brilliant in higher grades but also with something for 5 leaders. Avoid weekends when it becomes busy.	106
45 min	Lots of sun						A vast area providing superb stamina routes in an awesome setting. Route count only includes Barrots. Approaches to four other areas are described.	122
							Shorter routes than elsewhere but they pack a punch. Tufa-covered conglomerate rock. Go carefully at first as tendons will be tested to the limit in pockets of all shapes and sizes.	130
5 min to 10 min	Lots of sun				✓		Lots of routes and very convenient access. Not a place to climb if feeling a bit jaded.	134
2 min to 5 min	Lots of sun			✓	✓	Restrictions	Good routes at both ends of the grade spectrum but not a lot in the middle. Currently has access problems with some chopped bolts.	138
5 min to 10 min	Lots of sun	✓	✓				Fine area with excellent climbing on towering pillars. Lower in altitude so warmer. Shade late in the day. Multi-pitch and trad routes.	142
							The remotest area in the guide and a stern test of driving and navigation skills. An early start is needed for a day visit. Camping available but no facilities so buy all food and drink before driving up the mountain road. **BIRD BAN at Mola Roquerola.**	154
30 min	Lots of sun					Restrictions	Beautifully positioned crag with perfect rock. Powerful routes so go when fresh. Best routes are in the upper 6s and above.	156
30 min	Sun and shade						Some quiant pinnacles with a variety of routes. The best wall has some great hard stuff. Sadly most of the easy routes have been de-bolted.	162
Roadside to 5 min	Sun and shade						A sheltered valley with routes on either side. Fine range of easier climbs plus some quality mid-grade stuff in the shade.	166

La Mussara

Mont-ral

Arbolí

Siurana

Montsant

Vilanova de Prades

La Riba

Cogullons

Margalef

LA MUSSARA

Mark Glaister climbing *La primera de l'estiu* (6b+), Sector La Proa, La Mussara. *Page 43.* Photo: Highroglyphics.

The crags of La Mussara are an abrupt finish to a plateau which overlooks the Mediterranean coast of the Costa Daurada and are probably one of the best areas to become acquainted with the climbing of the area. Their prominence at 1000m above sea level will offer you teasing views of the crags as you drive up the switch-back road from the coastal plains trying to read the guide book and negotiate hairpin bends at the same time.

There are several crags which make up the area of La Mussara each with its own individual character and style of climbing and the routes in this area alone would be enough to keep anyone busy for weeks. All the areas have easy access and plenty of mileage can be had whilst enjoying the views and filling your lungs with the pine and herb-scented air.

THE ROUTES

White, grey and orange faces, seamed with cracks and corners, give dozens of wonderful climbs with a number of more adventurous multi-pitch routes thrown in. There are long crack lines reminiscent of some fo the more famous American venues, edges, corners, aretes and pockets galore. You name it, La Mussara has it!

The greatest concentration of grades is from 5 to 7a. The rock quality ranges from very good to excellent and often at a user-friendly angle. All routes are equipped with good hanger bolts or stonking great cemented bolts and usually have convenient chain and karabiner lower-offs. The older routes are gradually being re-equipped.

LOCAL GUIDEBOOK

A full list of the routes is available in the local guide. See page 6 for details.

CONDITIONS

The crags face between south east and west catching any sun that is going. They are often sheltered from the wind which blows over the top and consequently it can get very hot here. However, this area is the first elevation that any moisture coming up from the sea encounters and it can sometimes be shrouded in mist. When this happens, it is best to climb elsewhere. You will not find dry buttresses in the rain, but they do dry almost instantly when the rain stops.

LOCAL FACILITIES

The La Mussara Refuge is one of the best in the Sierra de Prades. You can camp and use the refuge facilities or sleep in the refuge. The guardians do a grand job of keeping the place clean. You can also buy meals and drink at the refuge. If you want to be self-sufficient, bring your provisions with you since there is no convenient shop near by. The intermittent water supply at the refuge may not be wholly suitable but the font on the way to the TV Crags is good water.

APPROACH

The crags of La Mussara are reached via switch-back mountain roads that climb up from Reus, Tarragona and the coastal plains. For the first time visitor the most straight forward approach is to take the N420 west out of Reus and follow this for 5km. Take a right (sign posted 'Maspujols') and follow this road (T704) through the small towns of Maspujols, l'Aleixar and around Vilaplana. Vilaplana is located at the base of the Sierra de la Mussara and the crags of Mussara TV will be visible overhead. The road now steepens for 5km and winds its way up to the parking areas for Mussara TV and the sectors of Isabel, Lo Raval and Lo Soterrani. In order to reach the refuge and the derelict hamlet of La

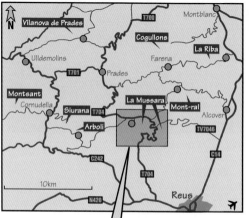

Mussara, continue up the hill following the signs for 'La Mussara'. The refuge is 5km from the previously mentioned parking area. Day parking is allowed free at the refuge which is the departure point for Les Campanilles.

Other less easily found but convenient approaches to La Mussara are:-
1) Via the C14 North out of Reus and left on the TV-7046, before reaching Alcover. Continue to L'Albiol and so onto La Mussara (this is the easiest drive up the mountain).
2) Via Alforja on the C242 and right on the TV-7012, sign posted 'Arbolí'. Don't go all the way to Arbolí but take the right turn (TV-7092) to Los Castillejos (a military camp). Go past the camp and reach the refuge turn off after 5km.

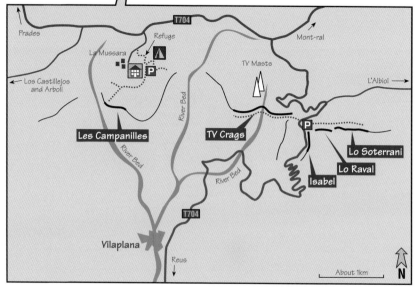

La Mussara

Mont-ral

Arbolí

Siurana

Montsant

Vilanova de Prades

La Riba

Cogullons

Margalef

Emma Medara on the groove of *El Canto de Gallo* (6c+) Sector Diedres del Mig at la Mussara. *Page 48.* Photo: Highroglyphics

TV CRAGS

La Mussara TV is one of the most important crags in the region. The line of sectors stretching out below the TV masts offer dozens of quality pitches set in a dramatic location 1000m above the Mediterranean. There is a good spread of grades and climbing styles on offer here although nothing much in the 'very hard' category.

APPROACH

From the parking area on the hairpin-ridden T704 approach road, walk northwards (towards the TV masts) along the road for 50m. Take a path on the left and the first crags are reached after 270m. Travel between the sectors is via a good network of paths but take note of the distances on the map above since it is not always possible to tell where you are when in the trees.

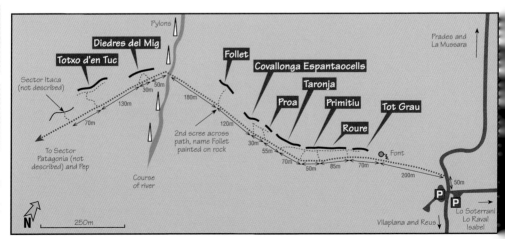

Pylons

Prades and La Mussara

Diedres del Mig

Totxo d'en Tuc

Follet

Covallonga Espantaocells

Taronja

Proa   Primitiu

Tot Grau

Roure

Sector Itaca
(not described)

50m
30m

130m

70m

180m

120m

2nd scree across
path, name Follet
painted on rock

30m

55m

70m   50m   85m   70m

200m

Font

To Sector
Patagonia (not
described) and Pep

Course
of river

50m

P   P

Lo Soterrani
Lo Raval
Isabel

Vilaplana and Reus

N   250m

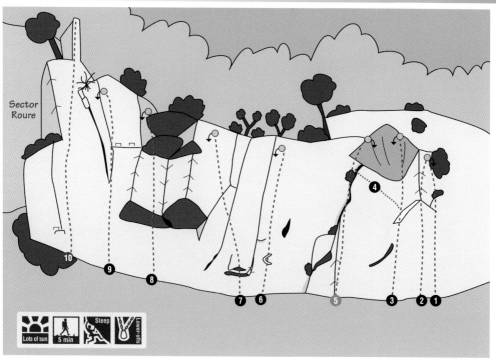

Sector Roure

Lots of sun | 5 min | Steep | Lower-offs | Slip-resistant

La Mussarra

Mont-ral

Arbolí

Siurana

Montsant

Vilanova de Prades

La Riba

Cogullons

Margalef

SECTOR TOT GRAU

Tot Grau is actually the first of the sectors that make up the long escarpment of Mussara TV crags but it is easily overlooked being fairly small and tucked away around the corner from the dominating wall of Sector Roure. Only a few of the routes on this sector are worthy of attention but it is worth a look if you are after a quick tick of a 7.

❶ Hola Forastero . . . . . 🔲 **7b**

❷ Me Quedo Aqui . . 🔲 **7a+**

❸ Tu Ordevas . . . . . . 🔲 **7b**
Start up the slab and then breach the large triangular bulge above.

❹ Variant . . . . 🔲 **?**
Head out left underneath the triangular overlap to finish up *Strip de Drap*.

❺ Strip de Drap . . . . 🔲 **6a**
Follow the crack/flake up to the left of the triangular overlap. The bolts are old.

❻ Noni . . . . 🔲 **7b**
A powerful series of moves over the starting bulge places you at the bottom of the fine crack which continues to the top.

❼ Invertits Divertits . . . 🔲 **7c**
Another powerful start, but it avoids the cracks above and ventures diagonally left up the rippled face.

❽ La utòpica . . . . 🔲 **?**
This just looks like a real grunt and graunch.

**❾ Ponte Bien que
te Conviene** . . . . 🔲 **7c**
A technical start leads to a rest at halfway. Continue up the crack line above.

❿ La Mussaranya . . . . . 🔲 **6c+**
Is this the equivalent of the *Cumbrian*, the *Northumbrian* or perhaps the *Devonian*? Even if it isn't it takes you all the way up to an impressive position right at the top of that pillar above you. No lower-off.

La Mussara

Mont-ral

Arbolí

Siurana

Montsant

Vilanova de Prades

La Riba

Cogullons

Margalef

The striking crack of *Aigua Viva* (6b) on Sector Roure. The crack to the right is *Roure* (6b).
Photo: Chris Craggs
Below

SECTOR ROURE

This brilliant sector is where many visitors to the Costa Daurada get their first taste of the climbing and it provides sustained and elegant climbing with some very strong lines. The cracks feel a bit granite-like in places and overall the rock quality is superb.

❶ Ones verticals 6b
Sustained climbing following scoops and a steep crack.

❷ Ariadna en el laberint grotesc . . . . 7b+

❸ Roure 6b
The fine right-hand crack has a hard, polished start.

❹ Aigua Viva 6b
The left-hand crack gives climbing reminiscent of granite. Another hard start. Suffering from over-climbing but still a good line. *Photo above.*

❺ Shargamanta 6c
Lovely steady crack climbing leads to a distinct crux. Once you have sorted this out, climb the left-hand crack to a mantelshelf finish.

❻ Kikanoune . . . . 7b+

❼ Jarias Krisnas 7b

❽ Cicatriz . . . . 7a+
Climb the first 10m of *Esduguardabaga* then break right up the remarkably sustained and varied crack line.

❾ Esduguardabaga . 6c+
Perfect wall climbing on slopers and small edges and a rounded mantelshelf finish.

❿ Tu no vadis 6c
Tough wall climbing leads to an easier finish up the suspiciously thin flake crack.

⓫ Namaste . . . . 7a+

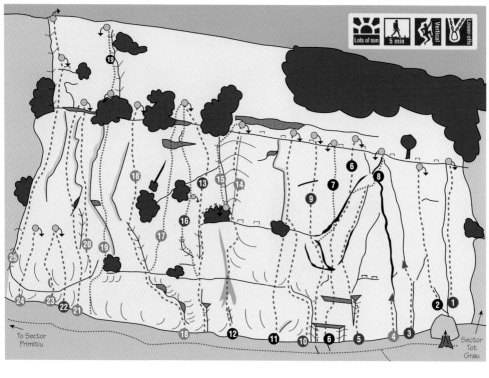

The routes on the left-hand side give some good long pitches.

⑫ Encarnación Fatal . . . 🔳🔳⬜ **7b**

**⑬ Saca la cinta
y vámonos** . . . . 🔳🔳⬜ **6b**
35m. A good sustained bit of wall climbing with the fine open groove providing the technical crux. There is a mid-route lower-off.

Two easy upper pitches are available to the right of the upper section of *Saca la cinta y vámonos*. They are only 5 but you need to be able to climb 6b to reach them.

⑭ Esperó del sol . . . . 🔳⬜ **5**
Takes the finely-positioned bulging arete.

⑮ Please Babe . . . . . 🔳🔳⬜ **5**
Direct up the corner.

⑯ Passió d'Esparraguera 🔳🔳⬜ **6c**
35m. A slightly unbalanced route with a very hard crux section through the overhang at the top.

⑰ Infierno de cobardes . . . 🔳⬜ **6a+**
35m. Break right up the fine wall after the initial layback crack of *Doll de lluna*.

⑱ Doll de lluna . . . . 🔳⬜ **6a**
35m. A good start and finish make this a very worthwhile route. It is slightly spoilt by a short broken section in the middle.

⑲ Formiga/El Gat . . . . . . 🔳⬜ **6a**
A wandering line.
1) 6a. Take care at the start. **2) 5+**

⑳ Lacònia . . . . 🔳⬜ **6a**
Nice sustained climbing all the way up the clean face. Watch out for the first clip.

㉑ Gesamí . . . . 🔳🔳⬜ **6a**
Steep moves at the start lead to much easier climbing above.

**㉒ Donde digo Diego,
digo dedo** . . . . 🔳⬜ **6b+**

㉓ So Far Away . . . . 🔳⬜ **6a**

㉔ Erespelma i zoide . . . . . 🔳⬜ **6b**
Rusty first bolt.

㉕ Esperó de Tardor . . . . . 🔳⬜ **5**
A bit of an expedition starting in the gully to the left of the bulging arete.
1) 5, 35m. Steep initial moves lead to easier climbing above.
2) 5, 10m. Very short and has a slightly loose finish. Descend by abseil from an anchor 10m right (looking in).

La Mussara

Mont-ral

Arbolí

Siurana

Montsant

Vilanova de Prades

La Riba

Cogullons

Margalef

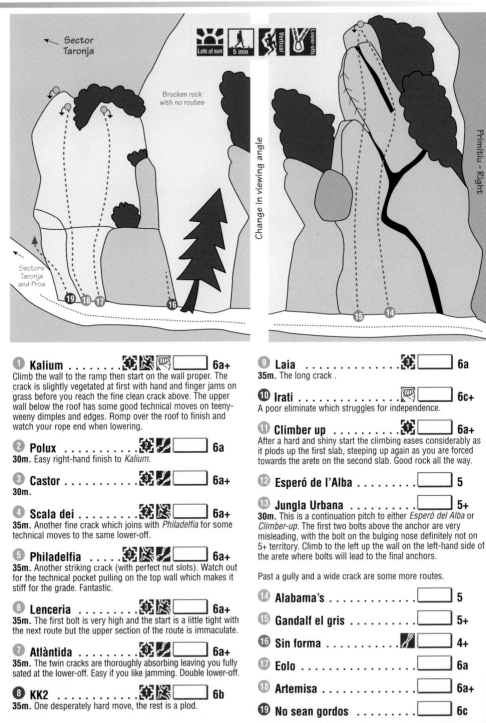

① Kalium .... 6a+
Climb the wall to the ramp then start on the wall proper. The crack is slightly vegetated at first with hand and finger jams on grass before you reach the fine clean crack above. The upper wall below the roof has some good technical moves on teeny-weeny dimples and edges. Romp over the roof to finish and watch your rope end when lowering.

② Polux 6a
30m. Easy right-hand finish to *Kalium*.

③ Castor .... 6a+
30m.

④ Scala dei .... 6a+
35m. Another fine crack which joins with *Philadelfia* for some technical moves to the same lower-off.

⑤ Philadelfia .... 6a+
35m. Another striking crack (with perfect nut slots). Watch out for the technical pocket pulling on the top wall which makes it stiff for the grade. Fantastic.

⑥ Lenceria .... 6a+
35m. The first bolt is very high and the start is a little tight with the next route but the upper section of the route is immaculate.

⑦ Atlàntida .... 6a+
35m. The twin cracks are thoroughly absorbing leaving you fully sated at the lower-off. Easy if you like jamming. Double lower-off.

⑧ KK2 .... 6b
35m. One desperately hard move, the rest is a plod.

⑨ Laia 6a
35m. The long crack .

⑩ Irati .... 6c+
A poor eliminate which struggles for independence.

⑪ Climber up .... 6a+
After a hard and shiny start the climbing eases considerably as it plods up the first slab, steeping up again as you are forced towards the arete on the second slab. Good rock all the way.

⑫ Esperó de l'Alba 5

⑬ Jungla Urbana .... 5+
30m. This is a continuation pitch to either *Esperó del Alba* or *Climber-up*. The first two bolts above the anchor are very misleading, with the bolt on the bulging nose definitely not on 5+ territory. Climb to the left up the wall on the left-hand side of the arete where bolts will lead to the final anchors.

Past a gully and a wide crack are some more routes.

⑭ Alabama's 5

⑮ Gandalf el gris .... 5+

⑯ Sin forma .... 4+

⑰ Eolo 6a

⑱ Artemisa .... 6a+

⑲ No sean gordos 6c

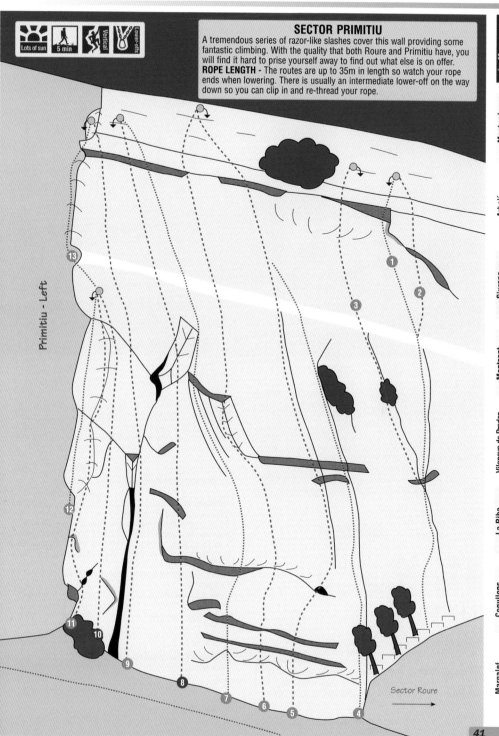

SECTOR PRIMITIU

A tremendous series of razor-like slashes cover this wall providing some fantastic climbing. With the quality that both Roure and Primitiu have, you will find it hard to prise yourself away to find out what else is on offer.

ROPE LENGTH - The routes are up to 35m in length so watch your rope ends when lowering. There is usually an intermediate lower-off on the way down so you can clip in and re-thread your rope.

Lots of sun

5 min

Vertical

Lower-offs

Primitiu - Left

La Mussara

Mont-ral

Arbolí

Siurana

Montsant

Vilanova de Prades

La Riba

Cogullons

Margalef

Sector Roure

La Mussarra

Mont-ral

Arbolí

Siurana

Montsant

Vilanova de Prades

La Riba

Cogullons

Margalef

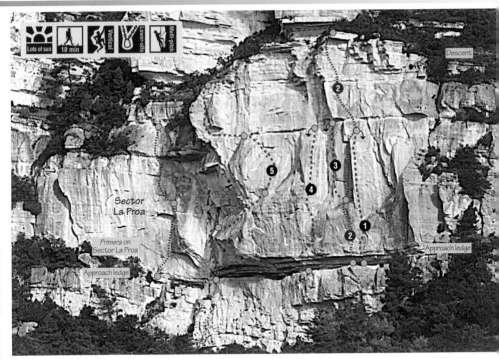

SECTOR TARONJA

The towering orange-coloured walls of Sector Taronja are an eye-catching feature of the Mussara TV crags. Many early routes were climbed on this sector and rusting pegs and old aid pitches are testament to that. Nowadays there are a few excellent multi-pitch expeditions as well as some hard routes. The routes listed here (except route 5) have good situ gear and modern lower-offs. The exposure is instant as you launch onto the severely undercut face from the starting ledges which are 12m above the footpath.

❶ Mare de Déu, quin pati . . . 7b
A very difficult pull over the overhang gives access to the sustained arete and wall above. The position is wild.

❷ Je ne se res d'alpinisme . . 7a
A great expedition up the longest part of the wall.
1) 6b. A strenuous feet-off start leads to some tricky face moves.
2) 7a. A good but demanding pitch which starts with some awkward bridging and ends with wild moves out right to the belay and a lower-off. At the top end of the grade.
3) 6c. A fine pitch again in a good position. Climb the line of bolts leading leftwards to a possible stance at two bolts in the corner. Make tricky moves up the thin crack in the steep wall to the left which leads to easier climbing and the top of the crag.

❸ Nice & Warm . . . 7b
A well-positioned arete. Start from the first stance of route 2. Note - There is a line of bolts in the corner immediately to the left of *Nice & Warm*.

❹ Amadeus . . . . 7a+
No details are known but it looks very impressive.

❺ Augusta . . . . 7a+
A long and classic route in a stunning position however no one seems to get beyond the first 5m. The upper pitches probably need new gear since the stuff currently in place looks dreadful. A full rack will be required. A good opportunity for the *trads* to show the *sporty-types* how it's done - no hanging around on the first few bolts though.
1) 7a+. Difficult climbing to a stance just left of the huge exposed slab.
2) 4+. Take the slab rightwards to a bolted stance where the roof above diminishes.
3) 5+. Up and leftwards to a stance at the base of a large corner.
4) 6a. Traverse left to the next corner and climb this to the top.

DESCENT for Routes ❷ and ❺
Walk 50m to the left (facing out) and locate some abseil anchors at the top of Sector Primitiu. Very prickly.

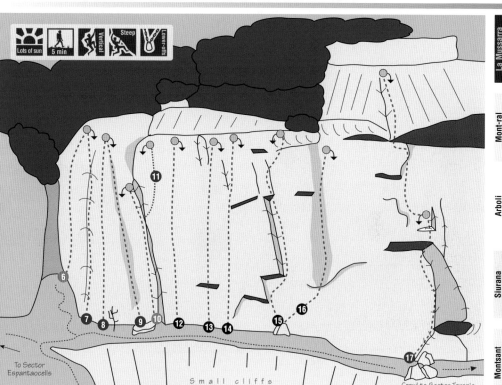

To Sector
Espantaocells

Small cliffs

Crawl to Sector Taronja

La Mussara · Mont-ral · Arboli · Siurana · Montsant · Vilanova de Prades · La Riba · Cogullons · Margalef

SECTOR LA PROA

This small sector has a handful of quality pitches ranging from the pocketed left-hand routes to the classic technical groove of *Obiang*. Other routes to try are the obvious *Chain Reaction* look-a-like, *Vol de nit* and the two pitch outing of *La primera del estiu* - but don't miss out on the other climbs as they are all good. It is sometimes sheltered when Roure and Primitiu are windy.

This sector is usully approached from its left-hand end hence the routes are described from left to right.

6 Carrasclet . . . . 🔆🔆 [____] **6a+**

7 Gallicant . . . . 🔆🔆 [____] **6b+**

8 Acuario . . . . 🔆🔆🔆 [____] **6b+**
Far more interesting than first appearances suggest as are all the routes on this wall. Easy initial pocket pulling leads to intense moves on the upper half.

9 Lastancio . . . . 🔆🔆 [____] **6b+**

10 Montsant . . . . [____] **5+**

11 Vol de nit . . . . 🔆🔆 [____] **6c+**
The Spanish equivalent to *Chain Reaction* at Smith Rocks. Intimidating for the grade with spaced bolts.

12 Comando Pernod . 🔆🔆🔆 [____] **7c+**

13 Amok . . . . . . 🔆🔆🔆🔆 [____] **7b**
Fierce, fingery and technical. High 7b.

14 Pimpirimpauxa . . 🔆🔆🔆 [____] **7b+**
Brilliant and precarious. Low 7b+.

15 Obiang . . . . 🔆🔆🔆 [____] **7b**
The obvious and appealing line of leaning grooves. An amazing mix of delicate, strenuous and technical climbing all leads to a wicked mantel finish. *Photo on page 4.*

16 Lo Patacó . . . . 🔆🔆🔆🔆 [____] **8a**
The lower half is very fingery and technical but with some great moves. This may leave you on the crux upper half having had no rest to speak of. Can you spot the stuck on hold?

17 La primera de l'estiu . 🔆🔆 [____] **6b+**
A fine little expedition which has good exposure, a sense of adventure (for a sport route) and a tricky finish. With a 60m rope you can do it in one pitch and lower-off as long as you take care with the rope-drag. There are a number of bogus bolts and lower-offs above the first stance. *Photo on page 34.*
1) **6a.** Climb the crack and over the roof on good holds.
2) **6b+.** Move left from the stance and up to the open groove splitting the roof. Work out the moves carefully, and then commit yourself to the tricky sequence through the roof.

LA MUSSARA *TV Crags - Sector Espantaocells*

La Mussara

Mont-ral

Arbolí

Siurana

Montsant

Vilanova de Prades

La Riba

Cogulons

Margalef

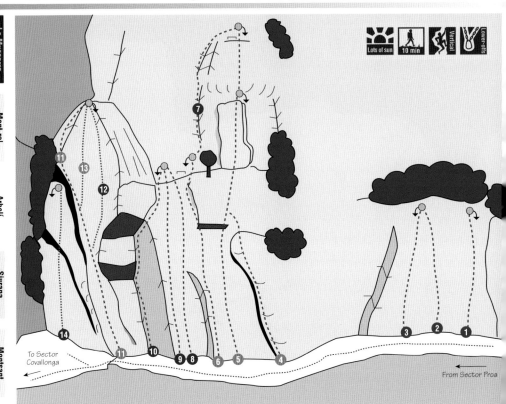

SECTOR ESPANTAOCELLS

This is not the best sector at the TV Crags but good for a warm-up or for some of the easier grades. The route *Espantaocells* is particularly worthwhile.

❶ Kora . . . . 🔆⬜ 4+
The first of three short 4s which are popular with beginners.

❷ Titànic . . . . 🔆⬜ 4+

❸ Tròpic . . . . 🔆⬜ 4+

❹ Això no és segur . . . . ⬜ 6a
The obvious bulging flake-come-crack.

❺ Espantaocells . . . . . 🔆🪧⬜ 6a
Easy for the grade with sustained and extremely pleasant climbing. There is an intermediate lower-off at the top of the detached pillar. The route continues above this for another 10m on steep ground but with good holds - 6b.

❻ Xell . . . . 🔆⬜ 5+
Climb the right-hand arete of the small, short corner.

❼ Sufre mamón . . . . 🔆⬜ 6b
A finishing pitch to *Xell* if you want it.

**❽ Me patinan
las meninges** . . . . 🔆🪧⬜ 6b+

❾ Pelut . . . . 🪧🪧⬜ 6b
It may look a bit of a path but some technical moves will have you thinking. Very nice.

❿ Me sudan los dientes . . . 🪧⬜ 7a
The large uncompromising roof-capped corner.

⓫ Equinocci . . . . 🔆⬜ 5+
Take care with loose pebbles when lowering off.

⓬ Pleniluni . . . . ⬜ 6b+

⓭ Solstici . . . . ⬜ 6a

⓮ El niño de Paquita . . . . . . ⬜ 6b

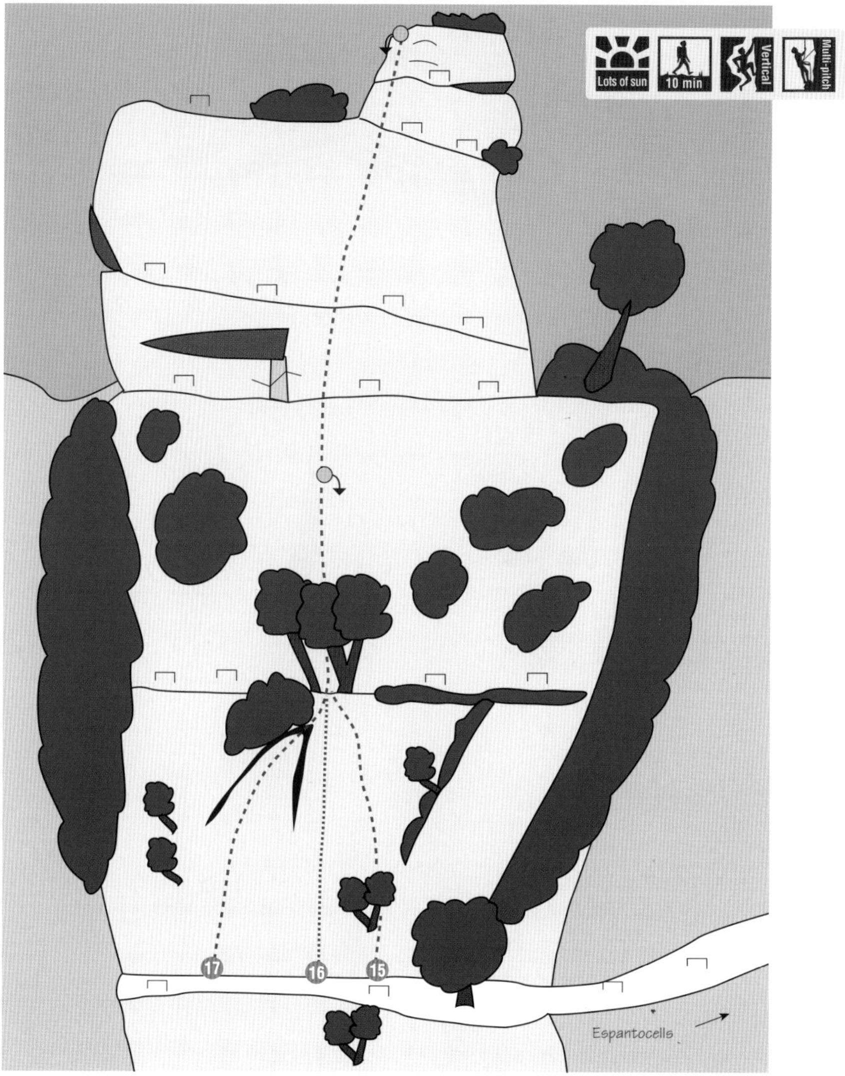

La Mussarra

Mont-ral

Arbolí

Siurana

Montsant

Vilanova de Prades

La Riba

Cogullons

Margalef

Espantocells

SECTOR COVALLONGA

A buttress with limited interest but *Covallonga* is a good 5.

All three routes meet at the first ledge at a cluster of trees and then continue to the top in a great position.

15 Sacallonga 5
Starts on the right-hand side of the slab just left of the vegetated groove.

16 Covallonga 5
The most direct way to the summit.
1) 5, 20m. The middle line of three.
2) 5, 15m. A good upper pitch well worth seeking out.

17 Facillonga 5
The left-hand side of the slab.

La Mussarra

Mont-ral

Arbolí

Siurana

Montsant

Vilanova de Prades

La Riba

Cogullons

Margalef

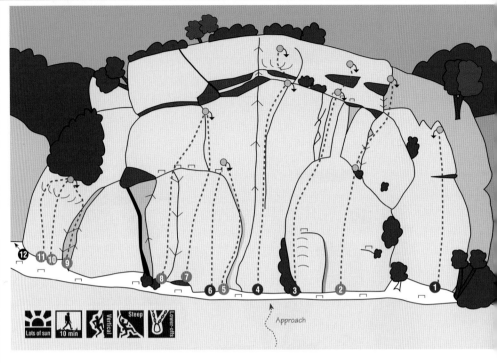

SECTOR FOLLET

From the footpath Sector Follet looks highly appealing; from the foot of the crag things take on a different appearance. However the overhanging crack of *Jarabe de Paco* is well worth making a detour for and while you are there, some of the other routes are worth a try.

❶ **Arrakatak** . . . . 6b+

❷ **Montse** . . . . 5+
1) 4+, 15m. Belay at the top of the broken slab.
2) 5+, 15m. Venture up to the anchors at the prow.

❸ **No sé cómo se llama** 6b
Scurry up to the start of the short crack. Do what is necessary and lower-off. The bulge above is a short 6b+.

❹ **Jarabe de palo** . . . . . 6c+
The main line of the crag is a striking overhanging crack right of the large arete. A good go-for-it attitude will get you to the top. There is a short 7a pitch above but it is best to lower-off here.

❺ **Delfos** 5
The climbing in the starting corner crack is okay but it abruptly ends with broken rock ledges.

❻ **Herme** 6b
The rounded slab is tricky to start but will soon ease as you reach the broken rock ledges.

❼ **Sara** 6a

❽ **Astanax** . . . . 5+
The broken corner crack.

❾ **Popeye** 6a
Do you need Popeye's bulging muscles for this one?

❿ **Pitufo** . . . . 6a+

⓫ **Makinavaja** . . . . 6a+

⓬ **Yosu Mubruto** 7c
20m around the buttress from *Maquinavaja* passing two large broken corners.

La Mussara

Mont-ral

Arboli

Siurana

Montsant

Vilanova de Prades

La Riba

Cogullons

Margalef

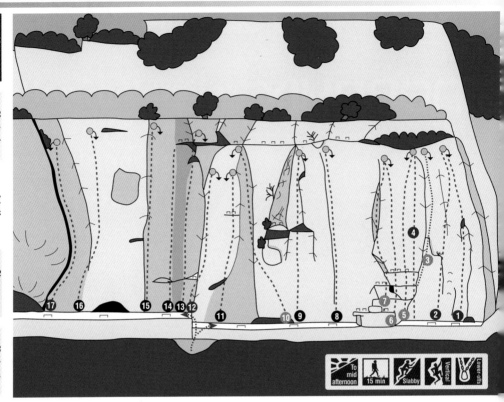

SECTOR DIEDRES DEL MIG

As you may have guessed from the name, dihedrals are a main feature on this sector as are the sharp aretes which jut out from the dihedrals. *El Canto del gallo* is a classic and should not be missed.

The right-hand side has fewer features and is more slabby.

❶ Fantasia rosa . . . . ▨▢ **6c**

❷ Truita de préssec . . . . . . ▨▢ **6c+**

❸ Desig d'estiu . . . . . ▨▨▢ **5+**
A great route following the series of hold-infested flake cracks which find their way to the anchors past one strenuous move.

❹ Xènia . . . . ▨▨▢ **6b+**
Very nice fingery moves take you up the lower section.

❺ Sis de deu . . . . ▨▨▨▢ **6a+**
A hard start leading to more fine climbing above.

❻ Chaoen conection . . . . . ▨▢ **6a**
The crux is the first step off the ground, after that you can settle back to enjoy the ride.

❼ Donantes de sangre . ▨▨▢ **5+**
A good pitch in quite impressive surroundings following the lovely curving open groove.

❽ Tendències suïcides . ▨▨▢ **8a+**
The thin crack. The rock all around looks smooth, so make sure your footwork is up to scratch. Not nearly as impressive as other 8s which can be found in the area.

❾ Psssh.... . . . . . . ▨▨▨▢ **7c+**
A pocketed bulging wall leads to the arete which is festooned with positive edges. *Photo on page 51.*

Photo: Highroglyphics

La Mussara · Mont-ral · Arbolí · Siurana · Montsant · Vilanova de Prades · La Riba · Cogullons · Margalef

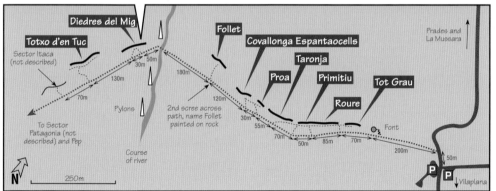

⑩ Jarto d'estar Harto ... 🔲🔲🔲 **6a+**
A brilliant climb taking one of the main lines of this crag.

⑪ Petirrojo .... 🔲🔲🔲🔲 **7b+**

⑫ El Canto del gallo ... 🔲🔲🔲 **6c+**
The arching orange corner is the most striking line. Interesting climbing leads you to the puzzling crux. To wall climb or to bridge? - that is the question. *Photo on page 36.*

⑬ Dinamita pa los pollos .... 🔲🔲🔲🔲 **7b**
The appealing orange and grey streaked wall.

⑭ Mr Farlop's ..... 🔲🔲🔲🔲 **7b+**

⑮ Largate d'aki ...... 🔲🔲🔲 **7a+**
A fine crack with the crux at the start.

⑯ Marta .... 🔲🔲🔲 **7c**

⑰ Eres un chulo .... 🔲🔲 **6b**
The corner crack by the huge bulging buttress is equipped with some very old looking bolts.

LA MUSSARA *TV Crags - Sector Totxo d'en Tuc*

La Mussara

Mont-ral

Arbolí

Siurana

Montsant

Vilanova de Prades

La Riba

Cogullons

Margalef

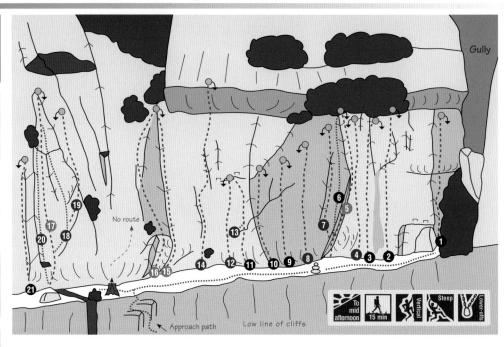

SECTOR TOTXO D'EN TUC

The furthest sector described at La Mussara TV has yet more good routes. Choose yourself a style of climbing and you will be able to satisfy your desire here. Some on the left-hand side are stiff propositions for the grade.

❶ Da Deus noces . . . . **7a+**

❷ Makibaka **7c**
Thin holds to the right of the prominent grey streak.

❸ Kiki . . . . **7b+**
Excellent climbing with great moves but slightly escapable. You would forgive the chipped hold if they had made it bigger.

❹ Petete . . . . . . **6c+**
A worthwhile route. Initial pockets and heart-fluttering moments lead you to the steep undulating headwall - the crack on the right at the top eases things up a little.

❺ Menjadits . . . . **6a+**
This rather brutal looking cleft is actually quite a pleasant route.

❻ Filosofastro . . . . **7a+**
A tight line.

❼ Angie . . . . **6b+**
A good route.

❽ Tec mac mayacon **7a**

❾ El gorrón de Bagdad . . . . **7a+**

❿ A santa compaña . . . **7b**

⓫ Entrada directa . . . . . **7a+**

⓬ Esqueixada sniff . . . . **6b+**

⓭ Estás a-kabau **6c**

⓮ Okemaka **7a**
This striking line is the first one you'll notice as you arrive at the crag base. The starting moves are thin and technical, whilst above lies some steeper climbing. A very good route.

⓯ Clean clan . . . . **5+**

⓰ Txop suei . . . . **6a+**
A fun and varied route.

⓱ Afrikan Regae **6a**
More sustained than it looks and with a stiff start.

⓲ Ojala Jalem **6c**
Same stiff start as *African Regae*.

⓳ Cuelebre **6c**
Do not use this as a warm-up since it is a bit gnarly.

⓴ Rastafari **6c**

㉑ Takashi . . . . **7a+**

LA MUSSARA *Lo Raval*

La Mussara

Mont-ral

Arbolí

Siurana

Montsant

Vilanova de Prades

La Riba

Cogullons

Margalef

Lo Raval

Lo Soterrani

Approach

Photo: mightygypms3

LO RAVAL

Lo Raval is a compact crag which will be of limited interest to most visiting parties since the climbing is sustained and the grades are on the mean side. The best way of sampling this crag is to double up with Sector Mosaic on Isabel Crag. This combination will allow the grade 6 climber to pack in a lot of mileage. The two sectors are about 10 minutes apart if the crag base path is followed (see maps).

WARNING - There is poison ivy on the approach walk.

APPROACH

From the parking area on the east side of the road, follow the obvious dirt road east for 200m. Just before the track enters the woods a path can be seen on the right. This is actually the bed of a small dry stream. Follow this south towards the cliff line. The path steepens and traverses along the tops of some small outcrops. Eventually the path forks, take the right fork and then the left fork at the next junction. The path now leads through dense undergrowth to the base of the sector in 150m.

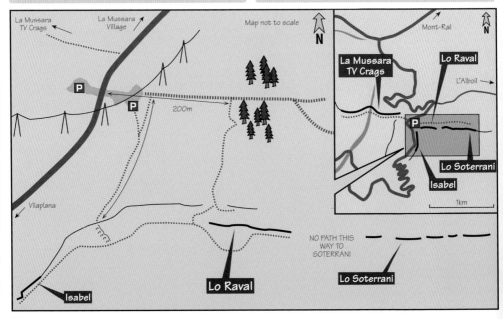

Mike Appleton on *Prisonero del deseo* (6b+) Sector El Biombo
Lo Soterrani. *Page 6?* Photo: Chris Craggs.

La Mussara

Mont-ral

Arbolí

Siurana

Montsant

Vilanova de Prades

La Riba

Cogullons

Margalef

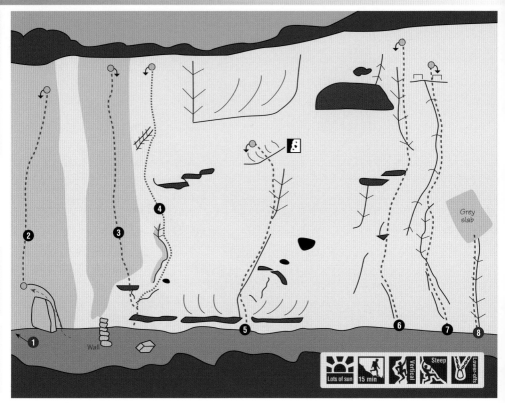

Lots of sun | 15 min | Vertical | Steep | Lower-offs

Grey slab

Wall

LO RAVAL

This section offers a good concentration of 7s and there is obviously potential for other new lines.

The first route is 40m to the left up the right-hand side of a red buttress.

1 Tot mundiellus . . . 6c
The rock isn't as appealing as the rest of the crag, but the line is impressive as it wanders up the ever steepening rock.

2 Yeti expres . . . . 7a+
Unlike many of the other routes here, the difficulties come higher up. Hard crux move.

3 El sebere berebere . . . . . Project

4 El signo de los tiempos . . . . 7b+
A fantastic line of shallow rounded grooves which twist their way up the peach wall.

5 L'Orxo 7c
The thin diagonal cracks in the orange rock make for some good technical climbing. Desperate moves to connect two pockets at the start.

6 Los reyes vagos . . 7b+
The mean start requires some teeth-gritting determination.

7 The hipotecaria . . 7b+
A prominent line following thin cracks, groove and the leaning arete. Escapeable at mid-height.

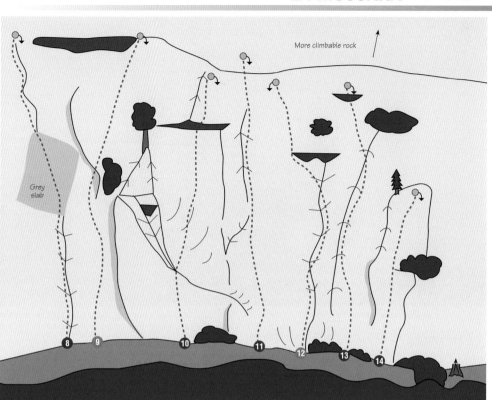

La Mussarra
Mont-ral
Arbolí
Siurana
Montsant
Vilanova de Prades
La Riba
Cogullons
Margalef

If you are just looking for a sampler, this is the end to aim for, the classic groove of *El Emigrante* being a sure thing.

❽ El emigrante . . 🔲🔲🔲🔲 □ **6b**
Superb climbing requiring a great variety of techniques so keep concentrating right to the top.

❾ Polos de gaseosa . . . 🔲🔲🔲 □ **6a+**
A technical start past the first two bolts soon eases to pleasant climbing slightly spoiled by the trip in the vegetation.

❿ Monopoli . . . . . . 🔲🔲🔲 □ **7a**
Remember your footwork for this technical piece of wall.

⓫ Kintros . . . . 🔲🔲🔲 □ **6b+**
Again the start will test you, but the difficulties keep coming. Great rock.

⓬ Rosa encarnada . . . . 🔲🔲 □ **6a**
The easiest route on this crag is well worth doing. Stiff pulls low down will get the blood pumping but you can soon get your breath back to enjoy the rest of the climbing.

⓭ Linea caliente . . . . 🔲 □ **6c+**
After some hard moves on numerous small pockets, the rock lies back as you head for the anchors.

⓮ Sueño erótico . . . . . . 🔲🔲 □ **7a**
Climb past a 'delicious' one-finger pocket.

LA MUSSARA *Lo Soterrani*

Mont-ral

Arboli

Siurana

Montsant

Vilanova de Prades

La Riba

Cogullons

Margalef

La Esquina del Viento (6c+), Sector Paret del Suís, Lo Soterrani. Mark Glaister climbing. *Page 59.* Photo: Highroglyphics

LO SOTERRANI

Soterrani epitomises the holiday crag - a beautiful situation, southerly sunny aspect and lots of great routes. The climbing tends to be off-vertical, only steepening to vertical and covers a good range of more moderate grades. Footwork is often the key to success, although finger strength will be called upon on the harder routes, as well as technique and determination. There are nice wide ledges to spread yourselves out on at the bottom of the crag and plenty of shady trees to lunch under.

APPROACH

From the parking on the east side of the road, follow the obvious dirt track for 400m. The track dips down hill through a wooded area. At the base of the hill take a right turn onto another dirt track and follow this for 70m to a parking area. (If you choose to drive this section go carefully, if it is wet, as the hill becomes slippery after rain). A small path leads south from the parking area (cairn). Follow the path for 450m, ignoring a faint track off to the right. The path leads to a descent down a gully which brings you out at the base of Sector Paret del Suis.

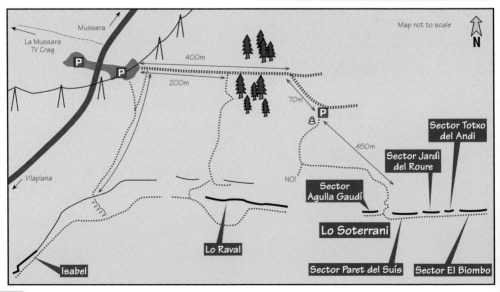

LA MUSSARA *Lo Soterrani - Sector Agulla Gaudí*

La Mussarra

Mont-ral

Arbolí

Siurana

Montsant

Vilanova de Prades

La Riba

Cogullons

Margalef

SECTOR AGULLA GAUDI

The first sector is on the right as you descend to the crag. The buttress is broken by some wide cracks and is not as good as the other sectors of Lo Soterrani.

1 Energía removable .... ☐ 6a+
The right-hand side of the buttress. It shares a lower-off with the next two routes.

2 Tipic d'aquí .... ☐ 6c+
A wall.

3 Espiritu burlón .... ☐ 7b
A shallow corner system. Start at a detached block and tree.

4 Calimba de lluna .... ☐ 6a+
A right-facing corner with a small roof at 4m.

5 La puta vara .... ☐ 7a
Start just right of a cave.

6 Stingo .... ☐ 6b
Start at the crack left of the cave and trend rightwards to a corner and over a roof to join the previous route.

7 Okeilusion .... ☐ 7b+
Start at the crack and step right onto the wall.

8 Encojonado .... ☐ 6a+
The widening crack to the right arete at the roof.

9 Llegó la llama .... ☐ 6b+
The narrow recessed buttress to a roof then left to a lower-off. Close to the adjacent cracks.

10 Stratocaster .... ☐ 6a+
The wide crack.

11 Pelea con la reina ...... ☐ 7a
The arete and flake above. A poor route since it is easy to bridge across and use the crack.

12 Cau de bloc .... ☐ 5+
Another wide crack.

13 Catalunya .... ☐ 7a
The wall to the left to a flake high up.

The last two routes are 8m left past some broken rocks and trees.

14 Now an Then .... ☐ 6c
The right-hand line

15 Cojón prieto .... ☐ 5+
Up to a shallow roof then right to the top. Hard for grade?

SECTOR PARET DEL SUIS

To get to the first route, turn left at the bottom of the gully.

16 Mala guilla .... ☐ 6a+
Keep to the line of the bolts.

17 Gen Gis Kan .... ☐ 5+
A climb of two contrasting styles; the lower section takes the slim corner flake/groove and the upper section takes the exposed rounded headwall.

18 Temperator ..... ☐ 6b+
The blunt arete is worth doing.

19 Flan Sinnata ...... ☐ 5+
A good route.

20 Pal mig .... ☐ 6a+
Finish up the crack.

21 Scarborough ...... ☐ 6b
Start up the crack then break out right onto the wall.

22 Pal fisura .... ☐ 5+
The crack all the way.

23 Mus d'atura .... ☐ 6b+
Fine climbing up the tricky corner crack and a wild layback up the flake.

10m

Paret del Suis 20m

Approach

Lots of sun   15 min   Vertical   Lower-offs

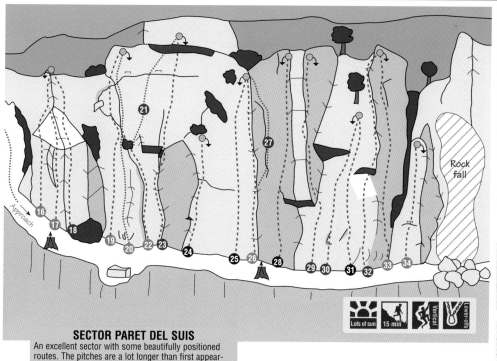

La Mussarra

Mont-ral

Arbolí

Siurana

Montsant

Vilanova de Prades

La Riba

Cogullons

Margalef

SECTOR PARET DEL SUIS

An excellent sector with some beautifully positioned routes. The pitches are a lot longer than first appearance suggests and are no push over either.

㉔ L'esquirol . . . . . . 🔳🔳🔳⬜ **7b+**
The overhanging arete leads to a dodgy lower-off (1 bolt & twig).

**㉕ Bartolo se
va al bolo** . . . . 🔳🔳🔳⬜ **7b**
An appealing but painful pitch which gets gradually easier with height gain. Make sure you don't have to redpoint this one.

㉖ Diedre del pi . . . . . 🔳🔳⬜ **6a+**
After tricky starting moves the crack provides excellent climbing in a great position. Hand jams and exposure all in a sport route.

㉗ La mora . . . . ⬜ **6b+**
A pointless route which involves climbing the crack in the right wall without bridging into the corner. Only do this when you have run out of routes. Same bolts as *Diedre del pi*.

㉘ Aresta Franklin . . . . 🔳🔳⬜ **7c+**
A desperate line on the arete to the right of the corner.

**㉙ La esquina
del viento** . . . . 🔳🔳🔳⬜ **6c+**
Take a good look at the spacing of the first bolts. Hard climbing leads to the magnificently positioned arete. *Photo on page 56.*

㉚ L'alhaja . . . . 🔳🔳⬜ **6c**
Steep and continuous climbing up to and over the dubious looking flake.

㉛ La tona . . . . . . 🔳🔳🔳⬜ **7b**
A good bit of climbing up the right facing flakes. Make a delicate step left at the top of the flake or face the consequences.

㉜ Asta de reno . . . . . . 🔳🔳⬜ **7a**
A badly bolted route. However a very long draw on the third bolt eradicates the heart flutter. The upper arete is very pleasant.

㉝ Avis-ala . . . . . . 🔳🔳🔳⬜ **6a**
Pleasant climbing on the left wall of the gully.

㉞ Interruptus . . . . ⬜ **6a**
6c without "canto sikado".

Right of *Interruptus* is a fresh rockscar which has removed the old route *Enel filo de la duda*.

La Mussara

Mont-ral

Arbolí

Siurana

Montsant

Vilanova de Prades

La Riba

Cogullons

Margalef

LA MUSSARA *Lo Soterrani - Sector Jardì del Roure*

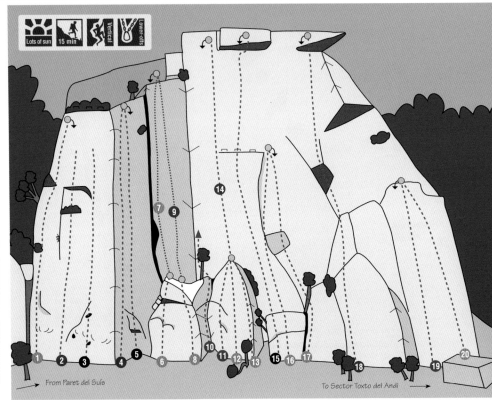

From Paret del Suís

To Sector Toxto del Andi →

SECTOR JARDI DEL ROURE
This sector has some fine face routes which are longer than they appear at first glance. Be careful when lowering-off.

❶ Aresta Guillem . . . . . ⬜ **5+**
An awkward start leads to a long slabby arete.

❷ Cabezón . . . . ⬜ **(7a)**
This is an unfinished route. There is a single bolt lower-off at the top.

❸ No val abada . . . . ⬜ **(7a+)**
Another unfinished route

❹ Todo tiene su fin . ⬜ **7a+**
A fine line. Fingery and technical climbing takes you up the never ending arete with stunning views. *Photo opposite.*

**❺ Sensibilitat
d'expressió** . . . . . ⬜ **7b+**
Very thin climbing. Wait until the shade cools the rock otherwise your feet and fingers will be screaming.

❻ La peluda . . . . ⬜ **6a**
Really only a start to reach the routes above.

❼ Love Without Frontiers ⬜ **6a+**
The obvious crack in the wall gives some sustained and excellent climbing.

❽ Que fa una noia com tu... . . ⬜ **6a**
Another way to access the headwall above.

❾ Exauri-Xell . . . . . ⬜ **6b+**
Solid wall climbing. Might be harder.

❿ Mal joc . . . . ⬜ **4**
Did you come to Spain to do this?

⓫ Kompresa con kanto . . . . . . ⬜ **4**
A means to an end to access the continuation route above.

Todo tiene su fin (7a+) on Sector Jardi del Roure at Lo Soterrani. Emma Medara climbing. *Opposite.* Photo: Highroglyphics.

⑫ Slumb 5
More of the same but harder. Can't complain about the rock though.

⑬ Jota Jota . . . . 5+
A thin start but things soon ease off.

⑭ En la cuerda floja . . . 🔲🔲 6b
32m. Climb one of the previous three pitches to reach the main event on this bit of wall. The climbing soon rears up with some blind and entertaining moves. Keep going and you will soon find yourself at the anchors. If you do it in one pitch from the ground then take care with the rope end.

⑮ El pez mas viejo del rio . . . . . . 🔲🔲🔲 7b
A slabby start leads to the impending headwall above. The middle of the headwall has some very thin moves but push on and you will end up in a spectacular position at the anchors. Watch your rope end when lowering.

⑯ Rhinolophus de terra dura . . . . 🔲 6a
After a slabby start you soon find yourself at the start of the much-steeper-than-it-looked-from-below flake crack. The holds are all there, so persevere.

⑰ El pinet . . . . 🔲🔲 6a
A short section of technical moves once you have stepped off the wedged block halfway up the crag.

⑱ Coraón de tiza . . . . 🔲🔲 6b+
Spaced bolts and discontinuous climbing, take some gear.

⑲ El nano . . . . 🔲 4
Short but on good rock.

⑳ La minyona . . . . 5+
Short, which means there will be some tricky moves.

La Mussara

Mont-ral

Arbolí

Siurana

Montsant

Vilanova de Prades

La Riba

Cogulons

Margalef

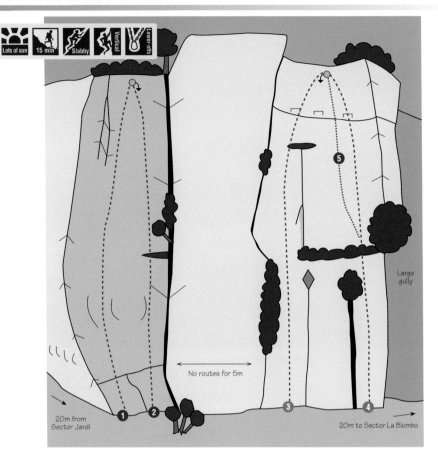

SECTOR TOXTO DE L'ANDI Y LA RAMPA

The first route of this sector is found 20m from the last route on Sector El Jardi del Roure, just after passing a large tree-filled gully. It starts just past the big bulging buttress.

❶ Camina Lucía . . . . . . 6b+

❷ Pandora 7a

The next route is on the slab 5m right starting to the right of the vegetated crack.

❸ Ali va bada . . . . 5+

❹ Mak Garra 6a

❺ Poc Garra . . . . 6b+

SECTOR EL BIOMBO

❻ Lo ticket 5
Run-out for the nervous leader. Go carefully.

❼ Lo teka . . . . 5+
An impressive route up the bulging buttress. The first 8m is climbed to the right of the bolts, almost on *Lo Taku*.

❽ Lo taku . . . . 5+
Start in the small corner and climb with care to the first bolt. Above lies some excellent and beautifully positioned climbing.

❾ Incha-la . . . . . . 6b+
The moves past the 3rd bolt are thin but lead to the fine arete above. Escapeable.

❿ Prisionero del deseo . . . . 6b+
A more sustained version of *In Cha La*. Good face-climbing. *Photo page 53.*

20m from Sector
Toxto del Andi

La Mussarra
Mont-ral
Arbolí
Siurana
Montsant
Vilanova de Prades
La Riba
Cogullons
Margalef

SECTOR EL BIOMBO

Another good sector with yet more striking lines. There are also some good trad lines which are well worth a look if you have a rack with you.

⑪ Panik-Haus . . . . . . 🔲 **5+**
The wide, vegetated crack. Not what you came all this way for, or is it?

⑫ El fariseo . . . . 🔲 **6c**
Desperate start.

⑬ Calcarius deliciosus . 🔲 **6b**
Worth doing if you have ticked the best. A bit of a thrash through the first bit of vegetation which then leads to some surprising and intricate climbing. Gets tricky when you least expect it to.

⑭ Multicrack sugestion . . . 🔲 **6a+**
If you've got a rack give it a go. No one else seems to have tried it in recent times. Can be top-roped from the anchors of *Calcarius delicious* if you are up to that route.

⑮ No me bellcostes la cuca . . . . . 🔲 **6a**
A fine pitch, saving the most difficult moves to the very last.

⑯ La tramantura . . . . . . 🔲 **5+**

⑰ Shalam Hassan . . . . 🔲 **5+**

⑱ Capitán Pedales . . 🔲 **6c**
The first of the striking lines on this section of the sector. A smart pull gives access to the thin crack and a testing move to the overhang. Don't mess up the first clip or you and your second's holiday will end right here. A wire is useful if you have one with you, the moves are about 5+.

⑲ La baraca . . . . 🔲 **6c**
A striking crack with a couple of bolts to start, then natural gear above.

⑳ Elegosentrick . . . . 🔲 **6a+**
Wall climbing (and a bit of wide crack climbing) at its best. A beauty. *Photo on page 57.*

㉑ Ben boig . . . . . . 🔲 **6a+**
Reminiscent of a Pembrokeshire classic? - well you can see the sea.

㉒ Keops . . . . 🔲 **7c+**
The hard route of the sector.

A hard new route goes up the wall to the right.

㉓ Aranja terrera . . . . . . 🔲 **6a**
A small rack is useful.

㉔ The talker bom . . . . 🔲 **6a**
A long and sustained expedition.

㉕ Madera de colleja 🔲 **5+**

LA MUSSARA *Isabel - Sector Mosaic*

La Mussara

Mont-ral

Arbolí

Siurana

Montsant

Vilanova de Prades

La Riba

Cogullons

Margalef

Isabel - Sector Mosaic

Approach scramble

ISABEL- SECTOR MOSAIC

The Isabel Crag is a large south-east facing cliff which has many routes along its rather broken length. Unfortunately most of the routes are line-less and are not of the quality found elsewhere in the Mussara area. The one sector worth attention is the Mosaic Wall which offers a few quality steep wall pitches. These are in the shade in the afternoon and could best be combined with a couple of routes on Lo Raval which can be reached along the base of the cliff line in around 10 minutes.

APPROACH

From the parking area on the east side of the road, a very faint path must be picked up heading roughly south (see map). The path improves after 30m and winds its way over old terrace walls until it picks up a dry stream bed. Follow this until it approaches the cliff edge and drops more steeply into undergrowth. At this point turn sharp left along the cliff edge for 25m until the metal rungs are spotted. Descend these and the fixed ropes to the base of the cliff. From the base of the cliff head downhill and bear right (facing out) along the base of the cliff for 150m to Sector Mosaic which is easily identified by the pleasant flat base and shaded picnic boulder and the first route name, *Didàctica*, clearly painted on the rock. (You will pass bolted lines before this).

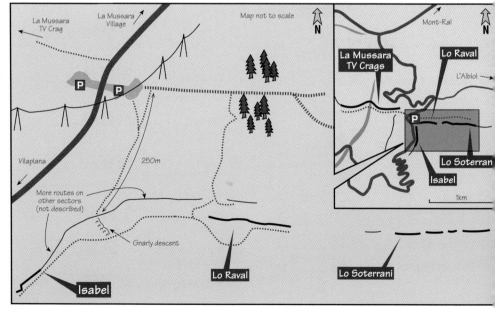

La Mussara TV Crag

La Mussara Village

Map not to scale

N

Mont-Ral

N

La Mussara TV Crags

Lo Raval

L'Albiol

P

Lo Soterran

Isabel

1km

Vilaplana

250m

More routes on other sectors (not described)

Gnarly descent

Isabel

Lo Raval

Lo Soterrani

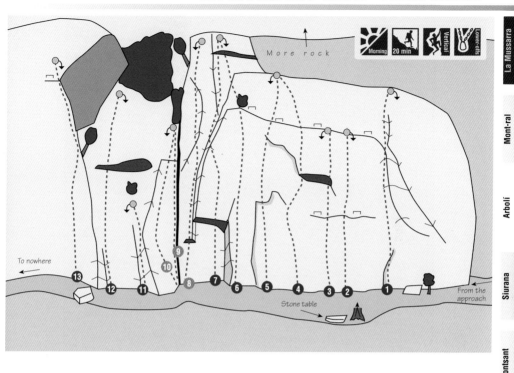

La Mussarra

Mont-ral

Arbolí

Siurana

Montsant

Vilanova de Prades

La Riba

Cogullons

Margalef

SECTOR MOSAIC

Stiff wall climbing and good views make this a pleasant spot best combined with a couple of pitches on the near-by Lo Raval which is easily reached in around 10 minutes along the cliff base (see map).

❶ Didàctica . . . . 🔳🔳 ⬜ **6b+**
A good pitch and quite amenable for the grade. Start up the obvious left-facing flake/crack after which good pockets are followed to the easier arete above.

❷ Cabrales . . . . 🔳🔳 ⬜ **6c**
A great piece of climbing and certainly no pushover.

❸ El sis doble . . 🔳🔳🔳🔳 ⬜ **6b+**
A ferocious start on very small holds leads to the half way rest. Above more difficult climbing on widely spaced but good pockets leads to the chains. This is only given 6a+ in the refuge topo but is as difficult as the other routes on this wall.

❹ Blanc i negre . . . . . 🔳🔳 ⬜ **6c**
The lower half of the route has some nice fingery climbing and you will soon find yourself picking your line up the wall by weaving from left to right, from black to white. It swings close to its neighbouring routes but manages to remain individual. The top black wall keeps the pitch a sustained one.

❺ L'àlfil . . . . ⬜ **6c**
Takes a line up the pillar which is a bit dubious-looking.

❻ Sonrisa vertical . . . . 🔳🔳 ⬜ **6c**
A great little pitch which requires a variety of techniques. It feels more akin to a trad route though and is slightly escapable.

❼ Tocata y fuga . . . . 🔳 ⬜ **7a**
The lower half provides the crux, the upper half enjoys the view.

❽ Skaramujo . . . . 🔳 ⬜ **6a+**
The climbing can feel a bit awkward at times but it is always interesting, varied and enjoyable.

❾ Only for Friends . . . . 🔳 ⬜ **5+**
The gaping corner crack in between *Skaramujo* and *El bloc de l'horror*.

❿ El bloc de l'horror . . . . 🔳 ⬜ **6a+**
A very off-putting name but pleasant climbing nevertheless. The difficulties are short-lived.

⓫ Dits de draps . . . . 🔳 ⬜ **6b+**
A short, difficult and unappealing line.

⓬ Stoykojo . . . . 🔳 ⬜ **6b**

**⓭ El negre
es tira de l'avió** . . . . 🔳 ⬜ **6c**
A very attractive wall from below, but once on the route you will discover it to be poor and sandy and it avoids the line completely at the top by bumbling up the ramp on the right.

LA MUSSARA *Les Campanilles*

La Mussara

Mont-ral

Arbolí

Siurana

Montsant

Vilanova de Prades

La Riba

Cogullons

Margalef

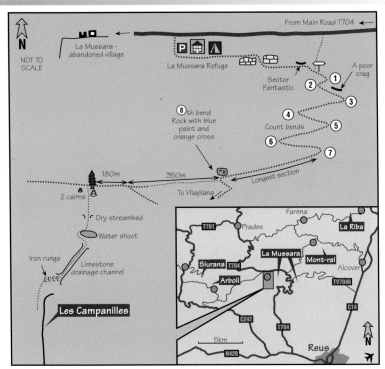

LES CAMPANILLES

A day spent climbing at Campanilles will leave anyone who operates competently in the mid 6s and 7s feeling totally sated. Although it has a longer approach than other crags, you will be rewarded for your efforts with quality routes that are long, sustained and absorbing. The lines follow long cracks or rippling faces and each has its own individuality and will hold your attention to the very last move. A feature of the routes on the main wall is the scoop. Each encounter with this scoop is as puzzling and tricky as the last, but all are entertaining. Once you know it's coming you will be ready for it, but it can have a clever way of spitting you out.

The routes are mainly concentrated in the 6b to 7a range and none feels particularly easy for its grade. Campanilles is a secluded west-facing crag and a visit there will probably be one of peace and quiet. The base of the crag is heavily tree covered which can offer respite from the hot afternoon sun. Now follow the approach to the letter and you will have a great day.

APPROACH

Park at the La Mussara Refuge (see page 35). Walk past the front of the refuge along a footpath. After 250m you will pass the tongue-in-cheek-named Sector Fantastic, a short crag with stuck-on holds (one reason why this is a selected guide). Another 50m will bring you to a footpath signpost. Follow the way marked 'Vilaplana'. The path becomes a series of switch-backs. Start counting the bends (including the first two short switchbacks). On the eighth bend, take a footpath which heads off right (west). **The footpath from bend eight is marked with a rock that has blue paint on it and an orange cross.** If you lose count, the section between bend seven and eight is fairly long and after bend eight, there are a couple of short switchbacks.

Follow this path for 350m through trees and vegetation, until it joins up with a dirt track. Where a track forks back left (east), continue straight on (west) for 180m, just beyond the end of the La Mussara abandoned village headland up on your right. Now take a small footpath left (south) at a small tree and marked by two cairns. Follow this for 70m until you come to a dry stream bed. Follow this downhill until you come to the top of a water shoot. Skirt around this on the right (facing out) joining back up with the obvious limestone drainage. Follow the course of this drainage until you can go no further. At its abrupt end there are some iron rungs, climb down these. At the bottom head left (facing out) around the bottom of the rock buttress. Scramble up to the ledge at the base of the crag via pruned trees and after 100m from the iron rungs you will arrive at the first route of the crag by the old dwelling.

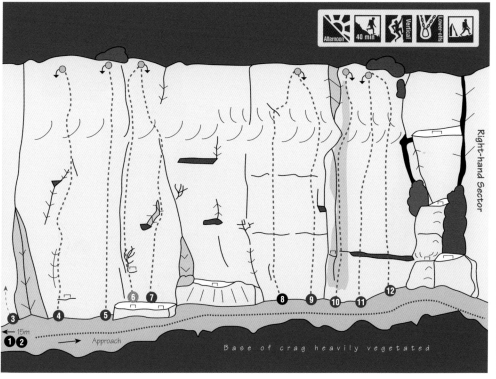

La Mussara

Mont-ral

Arbolí

Siurana

Montsant

Vilanova de Prades

La Riba

Cogullons

Margalef

LES CAMPANILLES

You've found the crag - well done. Now you can enjoy the excellent climbing and forget about walking out until the end of the day.

❶ La ley del deseo . . . . 🎟️🔏 ☐ **7c**
A fine route which takes the bulging buttress above the wall of the well maintained old dwelling.

❷ Marejadilla . . . . . 🎟️🎐🔏 ☐ **7a+**
30m. To see what this route looks like you've got to climb it. Unfortunately the chipper has been at work on the start but the rest of the climbing takes the rippling ice cream wall to the top of the crag.

❸ Amor vertical . . . . 🎟️ ☐ **6b**
The wall left of the crack. Lower-off at the roof.

❹ Zapatones . . . . 🎟️🔏 ☐ **7a**
The newest addition to the crag has steep and strenuous climbing and is a great outing from the word go. It is given 7a+ in the refuge topo but is a bit easier than that (which makes a change).

❺ Los elegidos . . 🎟️🎐🔏🎹 ☐ **6c+**
A series of long moves, rock-overs and balancy step-ups all leads to an encounter with the puzzling slopy scoop. Great climbing.

❻ Anda-lui . . . . . . 🎟️🔏🎐 ☐ **6a+**
Superb climbing up the striking crackline.

❼ Animal ferotge . . . . . 🎟️🎹 ☐ **6b**
All seems hunky-dory until you get to the scoop. Being at least 2m tall seems to be the answer here unless you veer off to the left or right. Happy riddle solving.

❽ Danone magarro . 🎟️🏵️🔏 ☐ **7a+**
Great wall climbing on sharp holds, brings the scoop within reach. Exiting the scoop yet again provides the crux which may need much to-and-froing from the good holds in the crack on the left.

❾ La bastonera . . . . 🎟️🎐🔏 ☐ **6c+**
A few long moves which require some thought land you in the scoop where you will need to execute a cross-hand move to reach the upper wall.

❿ No despistis . . . . 🎟️🔏 ☐ **6c**
The appealing grey crack is superb.

⓫ Mala folla . . . . . . 🎟️🔏🏵️ ☐ **6b+**
Only eligible for one star because it gets mighty close to the routes either side of it from time to time. Nevertheless, the climbing is quality and just keeps coming at you.

⓬ The Brothers . . . . 🎟️🔏🏵️ ☐ **6c**
A bulging start eases to vertical climbing, but still sustained.

La Mussarra

Mont-ral

Arbolí

Siurana

Montsant

Vilanova de Prades

La Riba

Cogullons

Margalef

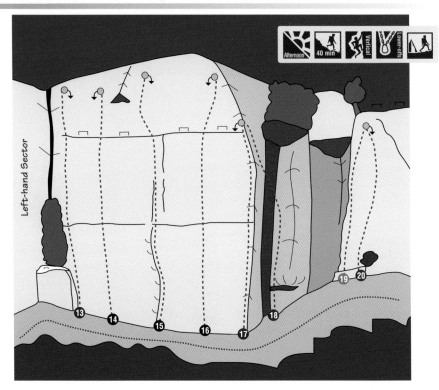

LES CAMPANILLES - RIGHT

The routes are less good on the right-hand side of the crag although the arete of *Sipegotimaato* is worthwhile.

⑬ S'ha morió er serdo ......⬚ 6c+
The poor line to the right of the wide corner crack.

⑭ Exta-sí ....⬚ 7c

⑮ Insí es lógica .....⬚ 7a+
This route can't make up its mind whether to be a crack or a face. Just as you plan to do a bit of crack climbing, think again and try some unobvious face climbing. Check your insurance as you launch off the big ledge, before the steep bulge, to get to the anchors.

⑯ Big-namba ....⬚ 7b
Head up the wall to the right of the previous route.

⑰ Visual persuasión .....⬚ 6c+
The obvious arete.

⑱ Entre bastidores ....⬚ 6b+

⑲ Sipegotimato .....⬚ 5+
The easiest route at the crag is well worth doing. The rock is good and the climbing sustained.

⑳ Kagando melodias .....⬚ 6b
Being only one of two 6b climbs at the crag you may choose this as a warm-up. Bear in mind that there is a good 6m section of sustained technical climbing, so you may prefer to do a few pull-ups on one of the many trees. The climbing is very good though, but you do have to weave around a bit.

The classic hill-top profile of the village of Mont-ral is easily identified from many of the roads that wind their way up, down, in and around the valleys of the eastern side of the Prades range. The cliffs themselves are tucked away to the south of the village centre and are not easily viewed from the road but offer routes of quality, in diverse settings, mainly in the easier to middle grades. Each sector described has its own flavour from the very open and route-packed El Riu sector to the impressive Els Gegants cliff with its selection of superb pitches. Another attraction is the potential for cooling off, or picnicking, in the idyllic river that lies in the valley bottom and is easily reached from the El Riu sector (early in the year only before the river dries up). Mont-ral would also make a good base for a few days for those without transport as all the crags can be reached from the refuge in the village.

Mike Appleton on *Calipso* (6c) on Sector Els Gegants, Mont-ral. *Page 77.* Photo: Chris Craggs

THE ROUTES

Although Mont-ral does not contain the same number of major routes as its near neighbour La Mussara, the routes have an individual stamp and the varied climbing styles will please most tastes. The first sector encountered on the approach described is Terranegra, not a very inspiring spot but it does give a number of shorter easier pitches useful for those just finding their feet or for a quick couple of warm-ups or downs. Much better pitches are to be found on the Arrepenjada pinnacle which is home to six or seven good easy grade 6s. The last two sectors included are also the most popular, and with good reason. Els Gegants has a great concentration of pocketed wall climbs and one superb two pitch 6c route up the very front of the main buttress. El Riu is a beautifully positioned sector with open faces and generally less steep pitches, again predominantly in the mid grade 6 range.

The Mont-ral area has many other crags dotted around the valley in addition to the four sectors described here; see the local guidebook.

LOCAL GUIDEBOOK

A full list of the routes is available in the local guide. See page 6 for details.

CONDITIONS

Although Mont-ral village is at an altitude of around 1000m, the crags themselves are lower and fairly sheltered being within the confines of the valley and generally south facing. It can become hot here but shade can usually be found at the base of the sectors, with the exception of El Riu which is more open and breezy. This area would not offer much climbing during wet weather.

La Mussara

Mont-ral

Arbolí

Siurana

Montsant

Vilanova de Prades

La Riba

Cogullons

Margalef

La Mussara

Mont-ral

Arboli

Siurana

Montsant

Vilanova de Prades

La Riba

Cogullons

Margalef

LOCAL FACILITIES

The village of Mont-ral has no shops or bars but the refuge is a lively spot catering for hikers and climbers. It serves beer and food and is open all year round. It also has a very good boot re-sole service. There is no camping at the refuge and it is probably better to camp at La Mussara Refuge, although people do camp on the football field (probably not advisable to leave a tent up here for security reasons). The nearest shops are located in the small town of Alcover at the bottom of the mountain, at the junction of the TV-7041 and the C14, the main road from Reus. There is a good restaurant off the crag approach track but it is not open often.

APPROACH

Mont-ral is most easily approached from Reus by taking the C14 north to Alcover (14km). Turn off the main road into the small town of Alcover and follow the signs for Mont-ral. These signs take you around the narrow streets and out onto a winding mountain road (TV-7041). After 12km the village of Mont-ral comes into view on the left. Turn left on the TV-7045, signposted Mont-ral. Another 1km brings a junction on the right which leads up to the village and the refuge. For the crags continue a further 250m and take a road on the left, which is signposted to a restaurant. Continue straight down the dirt road and park on the far side of the football pitch (200m).

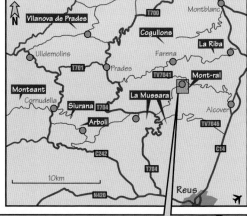

Mont-ral is also easily approached from La Mussara by taking the TV-7045 which is midway between the La Mussara Refuge and the TV crags parking area.

See map on next page for Sector approaches

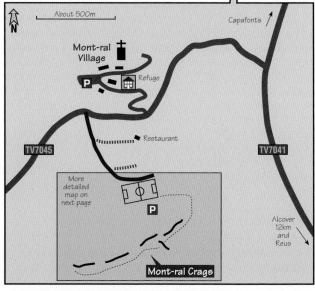

Solo para Ella (7b+)
Sector Els Gegants, Mont-ral.
Page 77. Photo: Chris Craggs

La Mussara

Mont-ral

Arbolí

Siurana

Montsant

Vilanova de Prades

La Riba

Cogullons

Margalef

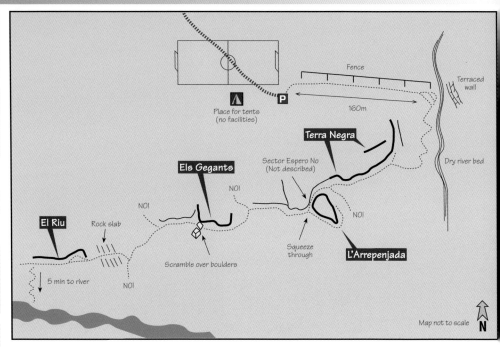

SECTOR TERRA NEGRA
This large and rambling sector does offer a good number of clean, easier-angled and low grade pitches. Certainly not the best routes here but useful for those just finding their feet or for some easy warm-ups.

APPROACH
From the parking by the football pitch follow the fence line for 160m to a dry stream bed. Drop downhill until the large face of Terra Negra appears on the right.

① **Cocoricó** . . . . [____] **3+**
Nice short slab. Unthreadable lower-off.

② **Tirabol** . . . . [____] **5**

③ **Tula, abdula, gandula** 🔆🌿[____] **5**
A good long pitch which can be used as access to the upper ledge.

④ **Comissari Negret** . . . . [____] **5**

The next three routes start from a ledge halfway up the crag. This ledge can be reached by a scramble in from the gully on the right-hand side of the crag, but it is over grown. The routes are best reached via *Tula, abdula, gandula.*

⑤ **Morros de llauna** . . . .[____] **6b+**

⑥ **Qui té duros, fuma puros** 🔆[____] **6b**

⑦ **Qui no té, fuma paper** . . .🔆[____] **6c**

⑧ **T'has cagat, que sí** . . . .[____] **7a+**

The rest of the routes are located on the lower buttress of this sector, down and left of *Comissari Negret.*

⑨ **El tio lila** . . . . [____] **4+**
Quite hard. Mind the tree on the way down.

⑩ **L'il.luminat** . . . . [____] **4+**
Slightly easier than *El tio lila.* Watch the tree again.

Espero No
(Not described)

Sector
l'Arrepenjada

Squeeze to other sectors

From parking

La Mussarra

Mont-ral

Arbolí

Siurana

Montsant

Vilanova de Prades

La Riba

Cogullons

Margalef

⑪ **Trossos grossos** . . . . 🔲 5+
This would definitely get more stars if it were longer, but what it lacks in length it makes up for in quality.

⑫ **Recoponostiofono** . . . 🔲 6a
Another short but very good route with a tricky little crux.

⑬ **Llamp de llamp** . . . . 🔲 4+
Good route with interesting bridging still quite tricky and technical in places.

⑭ **Yes fatu o faiste** . . . . 🔲 6a
A good sustained wall climb. Tricky move over the bulge.

⑮ **...i fumats** . . . . 🔲 5+
Bridging on to the tree is not allowed.

⑯ **Peus negres** . . . . 🔲 6a
Climb to the right of the wide corner crack and if you can keep from bridging you might make it 6a.

⑰ **Canal Pus** . . . . 🔲 6a+
Another route where you need to stick strictly to the line to make it add up to the grade.

⑱ **Not** . . . . 🔲 5+
A very bouldery and slightly polished start raises the heart beat. Good hard moves but make sure you get them right first go.

⑲ **Per la canalla** . . . . 🔲 4+
Pleasant climbing just before the entrance of the through chimney. High first bolt.

La Mussarra

Mont-ral

Arbolí

Siurana

Montsant

Vilanova de Prades

La Riba

Cogullons

Margalef

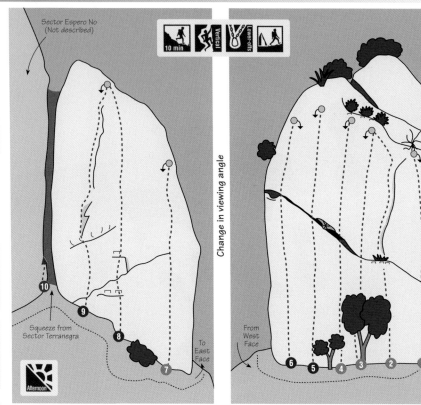

SECTOR L'ARREPENJADA

A good little sector which provides some sustained and well-positioned climbing. The two faces allow sun or shade to be enjoyed at all times.

APPROACH

From the left-hand end of Terra Negra squeeze through the obvious chimney. The west face of L'Arrepenjada is now on your left (facing out). To access the east face follow the path under the west face skirting around the bush.

❶ L'encagat de l'aigua . . . . . . ⬜ **5**
The short line on the right.

❷ Pandilla . . . . ⬜ **5+**
Take the small left-facing corner after the diagonal break and head up to the anchors on the left as for *La pastera del dimoni*.

❸ La pastera del dimoni . . ⬜ **6a+**
The climbing stiffens up after the diagonal break.

❹ Mala vida . . . . ⬜ **6a+**
You get yourself ready for where you think the crux might be only to find that it isn't there. A good route.

❺ El bloquieg del guaje . . . ⬜ **6b**
The lower wall warms you up gently for the stiff and sustained pulls through the bulge.

❻ Kin Kony . . . . ⬜ **6b**
Climb slightly to the right of the arete. Easier than *El bloquieg del guaje*.

❼ Yu yu . . . . . . ⬜ **6a+**
A route with a view, following the left-hand side of the arete on excellent rock connecting a series of positive edges. You can either start directly from below or by traverse in from the left.

❽ Ta . . . . ⬜ **6b+**
A great piece of climbing up the impending face.

❾ Rana . . . . ⬜ **7a**

❿ Gaston Rebotat . . . . . . ⬜ **4+**
The smooth sided chimney will definitely be a unique and one-off route in this guide. Your chance to do an unclaustrophobic version of the *Harding Slot* in Yosemite.

Calipso (6c) on Sector Els Gegants,
Mont-ral.
Photo: Pete O'Donovan.

La Mussara

Mont-ral

Arbolí

Siurana

Montsant

Vilanova de Prades

La Riba

Cogulions

Margalef

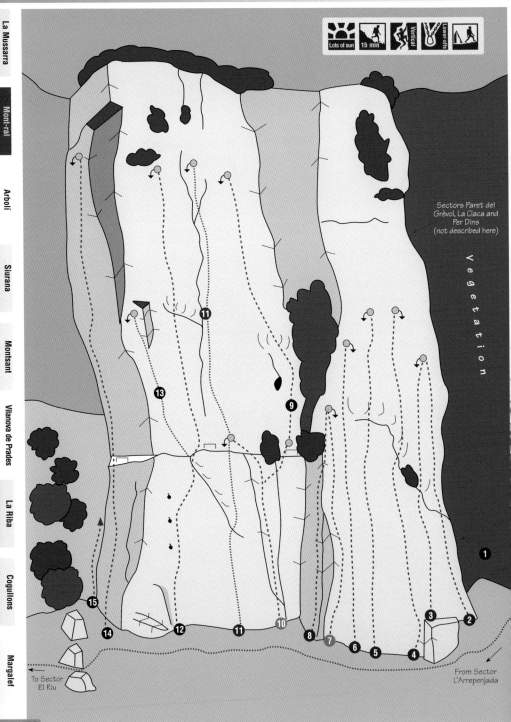

Lots of sun · 15 min · Vertical · Lower-offs

Sectors Paret del
Grèvol, La Claca and
Per Dins
(not described here)

Vegetation

To Sector
El Riu

From Sector
L'Arrepenjada

La Mussarra

Mont-ral

Arbolí

Siurana

Montsant

Vilanova de Prades

La Riba

Cogullons

Margalef

SECTOR ELS GEGANTS

Sector Els Gegants is the south-facing front wall of a large detached pillar. The climbs described here are some of the best for their grade at Mont-ral.

APPROACH

From the squeeze-through on l'Arrepenjada follow the base of the cliff line to the next large buttress and drop down to gain the front face.

SHADY SIDE - The back side of the pinnacle is a shady face (Sector Per Dins). This has a number of routes that would be useful should the south-facing sectors become unbearably hot. The best of these is:

❶ Foc als dits . . . . . 7b+
40m. A huge single pitch which is one of the best routes at Mont-ral. The name is painted faintly at the base and the route has big bolts.

The other routes on this wall are between 6b+ and 7b.

The opposite wall to Sector Pers Dins is Sectors Paret del Grèvol (left) and La Claca (right). The routes on these two sectors are between 6a+ and 7a+.

Back on the main wall.

❷ Wötsch Txitxa 6c
Don't miss this climb which is tucked away on the right.

❸ Eslava . . . . 6b+
Generous pockets appear at regular intervals making sure you can keep under control. If you are here at the right time, you can stop and munch on a fig at the midway break. Reasonable for the grade and good too (the figs and the climb).

❹ Réquiem per un Volvo 6c+
28m. Similar to *Calipso* and very worthwhile.

❺ Calipso 6c
30m. The best route on this wall. A sustained sequence of technical climbing on the initial wall leads to some more pumpy pocket pulling on the steep bulge above.
Photos page 69 and 75.

**❻ No em toquis
el pitu, que m'irritu** 6b
The lower orange wall is infested with huge jugs. The upper bulge is uncharacteristic and leads you upwards on flatties which bring on the pump rather quickly, so be positive, get well chalked up and climb with haste.

❼ Derribus i enderrocus . . . 6a+
The last short route on this section of rock which is not as good as the routes to the right. Nevertheless it is still worthwhile.

❽ Najarkala 6c

❾ Deponga su actitú . . . 7c
This route starts midway up the crag. It is best reached by climbing *Setciències* and then wndering over right to a ledge to belay.

❿ Setciències 6a
The initial moves provide the technical crux and nice climbing follows on generous jugs. You could nip up this pitch to get to the second pitch of *El problema de la gula* before the other climber starting up pitch one of *El problema de la gula* does.

⓫ El problema de la gula 6c
A fantastic route which, if climbed in one long long pitch, will be a sure test for any stamina lord. This is not just because of the nature of the climbing, but the rope drag and the weight of your excessive amount of quickdraws will be teaming up with gravity to pull you off. Therefore it is best done in two pitches.
1) 6c, 15m. Follow good pockets up the wall to a step right around the bulging arete. Continue directly up the arete via a hidden pocket to the anchors and belay ledge.
2) 6c, 30m. A brilliant pitch climbing the crack line above the belay which feels very long and incredibly sustained and doesn't ease until you've clipped into the final anchors. Locally this pitch is called *Aquí vé el dilema* and graded 7a+.

⓬ Sólo para ella . . . . . . 7b+
38m. An exercise in picking the right sequence of pockets on the lower bulging wall, followed by a good rest and well-positioned easier climbing on the upper wall. Think about taking 18 quickdraws as the bolts in the upper wall are very closely spaced or just miss some out. Low in the grade.
Photo page 71.

⓭ Alamut 7b
Another tremendous pitch sharing the same start to *Sólo para ella*. The crux is hard for the short.

⓮ Isidru . . . . 7b+
30m. A thin crack to start (hard) leads to a no-hands rest. Surmount the bulge above on jugs then climb the upper wall with increasing difficulty.

⓯ Mister Natural 7b
Up the slope.

La Mussarra

Mont-ral

Arbolí

Siurana

Montsant

Vilanova de Prades

La Riba

Cogullons

Margalef

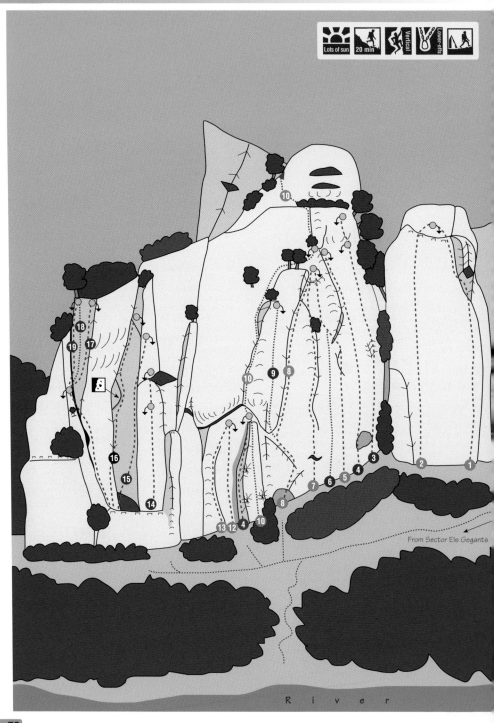

Lots of sun | 20 min | Vertical | Lower-offs

From Sector Els Gegants

River

Sector El Rui
Photo: Highroglyphics

La Mussarra

Mont-ral

Arbolí

Siurana

Montsant

Vilanova de Prades

La Riba

Cogullons

Margalef

SECTOR EL RIU
A large south-facing sector with a multitude of good long grade 6 pitches. The river is tantalisingly close and can be quickly reached for a cooling-off session.

APPROACH
Once you have scrambled over the boulders below Els Gegants, follow the approach map on page 72 as there are a couple of misleading paths on the route.

1 Pedreres a la merda . . . . . . ☐ **6a**

2 Arramba i clava . . . . ☐ **6a+**

3 Ronyons Invertis . . . . . . ☐ **6b+**
A series of bulges with small holds and good rock. A good route. The extension over the top bulge is 6a+.

4 Gos salvatge . . . . ☐ **6b**
Pleasant climbing with nothing particularly hard.

5 Sobredosi de couldina ☐ **6a+**
A good long route.

6 Neferkikis . . . . ☐ **6b+**

7 Piu-piu . . . . ☐ **5+**
A really enjoyable climb with lots of lovely jugs throughout.

8 Jolly Jumper . . . . . ☐ **6a**
This route was first climbed in 1980 and takes the striking corner to the right of the rounded white arete. The corner is surprisingly steep but bridging can quickly solve any problems that may arise if you are beginning to feel a bit strung-out.

9 Je suis pillé . . ☐ **6c+**
A striking line which has some very tough climbing in its relatively short length.

10 Romaní màgic . . . . ☐ **5+**
1) 4+, 12m. The right-hand side of the pinnacle. Bolted.
2) 5+, 20m. The corner directly above requires gear.
2) 4+, 20m. All the way to the top.

11 Aresta Bruts . . . . ☐ **4**

12 Potents i pudents . . . . . ☐ **6a+**
A more sustained climb than its left-hand neighbour.

13 Gamarús . . . . ☐ **6a+**
The crack is really very easy and the crux move is going for the finishing holds rather than grabbing the chains.

14 Perskindol . . . . ☐ **6c+**
An unsatisfying test-piece which ends abruptly half way up the crag. Above the first lower-off the route continues up on a series of shiny slopers at a hard 7b.

15 Kk's Crack . . . . ☐ **6c**
The appealing thin crack in the wall gives a great pitch which demands jamming skills when you least expect them. It can be slippery when hot.

16 Zimbawe . . . . ☐ **7a+**
The intimidating leaning corner is as awesome as it looks. This would be a 3 star route were it not for the 'wedged death-flake' at half height. Go very carefully with this.

17 Nasío pa volá . . . . ☐ **6b+**
1) 5, 25m. The obvious crack bounding the left-hand side of the crag to a belay on the left just after passing the overhanging arete on the right.
2) 6b+, 18m. Move out rightwards with feet just above the airy arete. Spectacular.

18 El boig del muntanyó . . . ☐ **6c+**
Starts from the first stance of *Nasío pa volá*.

19 Se chupa por la parte... . ☐ **6b**
Starts from the first stance of *Nasío pa volá*.

ARBOLI

La Mussara

Mont-ral

Arbolí

Siurana

Montsant

Vilanova de Prades

La Riba

Cogullons

Margalef

The main face of El Falco. Photo: Pete O'Donovan

The crags near the charming village of Arbolí are not as well known as those of La Riba, Mussara or Siurana but the quality, if not the quantity, is no less. The environment is tremendous with eagles and eagle owls (el duc) a regular feature and the views of Siurana and Montsant are breath-taking.

The two main areas described here are the Roadside Crags near the village of Arbolí, and the magnificent buttress of El Falco which is home to some of the longest single pitches to be found in the guide and is one of the major crags catering for those climbing in upper 6s and mid 7s. The Roadside Crags offer a wider selection of grades and are a good venue for parties with a variety of abilities. The climbing on all the sectors described requires stamina, good technique and finger strength. The rock is superb and the belay ledges beneath the crags very comfortable.

The village of Arbolí is a smart little spot, popular as a weekend venue for city folk and climbers alike. The refuge is basic but for those without transport it is ideal as all the crags can be reached on foot. For those wishing to make this a base there are several other sectors in the area, details of which are in the local guidebook.

THE ROUTES

Stamina is an essential requirement for the majority of the routes described in this area. From the leaning walls and crisp faces of the Roadside Crags to the neck-

LOCAL GUIDEBOOK

A full list of the routes is available in the local guide. See page 6 for details.

craning 14 bolt mega-pitches at El Falco, the tension will build as the distant anchors come closer and the thought of having to red-point what has gone before becomes too much to contemplate. The routes at El Falco are by necessity a little run-out, but the gear is solid. Much care is needed when lowering or cleaning the routes of quickdraws as many of the pitches are 40m long and will require a mid station lower-off.

La Mussarra

Mont-ral

Arbolí

Siurana

Montsant

Vilanova de Prades

La Riba

Cogullons

Margalef

CONDITIONS

The crags of Arbolí are at a similar altitude to those at Siurana but the area does not share its variation in aspect. All of the sectors described are in the sun from midday onwards, but are also fairly open and can often have a pleasant breeze. Consequently on cold and windy days it would be better to search out a more sheltered spot. If it has been wet it may be muddy on the approach road to El Falco so be prepared to park in alternative pull-offs and walk before you become stuck.

APPROACH

From Reus - Take the N420 west out of Reus. After 8km turn right to Bourges del Camp on the C242. Continue through Alforja to the Coll d'Alforja (10km) and turn right at the col summit on the TV-7012, signed Arbolí. Follow this for 5km to the village of Arbolí from where the relevant crag approaches are described.

From La Mussara - Arbolí can be quickly reached from La Mussara and Mont-ral via the TV7092, passing the Military camp of Los Castillejos.

From Siurana - From Cornudella follow the C242 south for about 2km. Turn left towards *El panta de Siurana.* Just before reaching the reservoir, turn steeply right and follow a winding road to the parking below Can Simiro.

LOCAL FACILITIES

Arbolí has a shop a bar and a restaurant. The shop is only open on Wednesdays and Saturdays.
The refuge is on the main street leading through the village next to the church. There is no camping at Arbolí. Potable water is available at the font which appears to come from the swimming pool! There is also a public phone in the square.

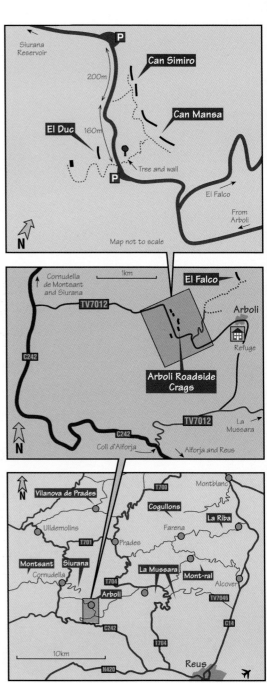

La Mussarra

Mont-ral

Arboli

Siurana

Montsant

Vilanova de Prades

La Riba

Cogullons

Margalef

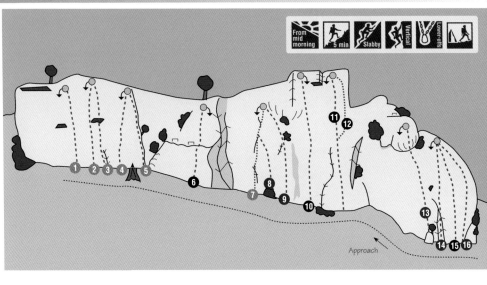

ARBOLI ROADSIDE CRAGS
The Roadside Crags of the Arbolí area are easily accessed and have a good range of grades. Most visiting parties will have a great day out.

The climbs on the Can Mansa sectors are suitable for those wanting an easy day or a few steady warm-ups.

The routes on the Can Simiro sectors are something a bit more special. The right-hand sector has a handful of quality face routes with *Esperó* and *Allegro man no tropo* being the best. There are also a number of good routes on the left-hand sector on steep rock with good holds.

APPROACH
The parking spot is about 1.65km south west from Arbolí village at a bend in the road. If these spots are full further parking is available 200m along the road on the right. These spots can also be approached from the other direction via the reservoir. Can Mansa is approached via a path that is directly opposite the parking pull-off, the path climbs steeply through the woods to the sectors in a few minutes. To approach the Can Simiro sectors walk north along the road (away from Arbolí village) for 110m until just beyond some large boulders on the right. Locate a faint path that leads up through the woods to the base of the sectors in a few minutes.

SECTOR CAN MANSA - LEFT
On first appearances things may seem a bit short but some of the routes are definitely worthwhile.

1 Guiri-gri . . . . 🔲 **6a**

2 Kuriosillo . . . . . . 🔲 **6a+**
Very hard and fingery route. Nice climb.

3 Marfullenga . . . . 🔲 **6a**
Excellent route. Big moves between positive holds. A bit like climbing indoors.

4 Domenec's patapumba . . . . . . 🔲 **6a**
One of the more interesting pitches on this little wall. Sustained all the way to the lower-off.

5 Iosumite . . . . 🔲 **6a**
Not quite Yosemite, but not bad. Pumpy

6 ? . . . . 🔲 **?**
A poor looking route.

7 Nosespande . . . . 🔲 **5+**
A tricky start gives access to much easier climbing.

8 Botifarra a seques . . . . . 🔲 **6b+**
Move into *Nosespande* at the third bolt.

9 Lolo flores . . . . . 🔲 **6c+**
Thin moves at the start.

10 L'avi . . . . . . 🔲 **7b+**
A fine piece of wall climbing taking the steepest and most sustained line up the white wall.

11 Carmina Burana . . . . 🔲 **7b**

12 Desvariant-la . . . . 🔲 **7a+**

13 Ja t'hi cagues . . . . 🔲 **7a**

14 Amanita Martinez . . . 🔲 **6c**
Technical and interesting moves make this worthwhile.

15 Endivia Cochina . . 🔲 **7a+**

16 Aixó s'avisa . . . . 🔲 **6c**
Escapable climbing.

SECTOR CAN MANSA - RIGHT

Many climbers visiting the Arbolí Roadside Crags only get this far, and then dismiss the whole lot. Don't - some of these are actually okay if only as a warm-up for the routes on Sector Can Simiro, and also for those seeking out easier grades.

⑰ Cabras rocosas . . . . . . 🔳 ⬜ **6a+**
The furthest left-hand route has some technical slabby moves and a pull over the little overlap at the top.

⑱ Patxanca . . . . 🔳 🔳 ⬜ **7a**
The middle of these three routes is technical in its lower half with fingery moves above the slabby ledge.

⑲ Moltes grasses . . . . . . 🔳 ⬜ **6b**
The convenient tree at the start of the route gets you on your way. Above the climbing is very good and totally absorbing to the very last move.

⑳ Escanya . . . . ⬜ **4+**
Bridge inside the crack.

㉑ Canti di plasti . . . . ⬜ **4+**
Climb on the right-hand side of the wide crack, crossing it at the top to share the anchors of the previous route. Powerful moves required on the top half of the route. The living end of 4+.

㉒ Valdric . . . . ⬜ **5**
Easy start leads to hard and polished climbing above making for a difficult and mediocre route.

㉓ Ninot . . . . 🔳 ⬜ **5**
Really interesting moves.

㉔ Feber . . . . 🔳 ⬜ **4+**
Hard start leads to nice climbing above.

㉕ Famobil . . . . 🔳 ⬜ **4**
Hard start and high 1st bolt make for a very bold opening. Otherwise nice climbing up the crack with a good layback.

㉖ E.H Sukarra . . . . 🔳 ⬜ **6a**
A very nice line with good climbing all the way up the curving groove and some great moves on brilliant big holds as you head right from the ledge to the anchors.

㉗ Cuencame un cuenco . 🔳 🔳 ⬜ **6c+**
The barrel buttress has compact rock providing the fingery crux moves of this route.

La Mussarra

Mont-ral

Arboli

Siurana

Montsant

Vilanova de Prades

La Riba

Cogullons

Margalef

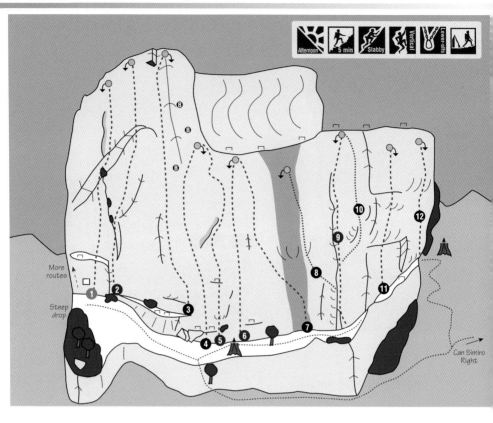

More routes

Steep drop

Steep drop

Can Simiro Right

SECTOR CAN SIMIRO - LEFT
A most appealing piece of rock which leans gently for most of its length. It is home to some excellent, long, sustained and pumpy routes, many of which are very onsightable.

There are bolts on a poor grade 5 the left of the first route.

1 The Mighty Pennis 6a
Start by the plaque and conquer the massive phallus. A poor route.

2 ? .... 6b+
Although the rock quality isn't as good as other routes, this long route is very enjoyable. The fingery crux sequence is only short.

3 Pa d'agla 7b
The route of the crag which is steep and sustained in its lower section. The first few moves are difficult to read. Higher up, things are easier (if you like slabs!). 33m long so take care when lowering off. There is a midway lower-off.
Photo opposite and on page 15.

4 Alambrado sea dios . 7b+
A stamina pitch chocka with good moves.

5 No m'enganyis més .. 7a
Steep climbing on good holds until the last few moves. Don't worry, take a breather and work it out.

6 Agua de fuego 7a
More fun up the steep white bulge. Have you tried the local tipple?

7 Ke te kalles .... 7a+
Desperate boulder move crux.

8 Inversió tèrmica 7b
Move out left from the base of *Catacrac*.

9 Catacrac 7a
The fine bulging thin crack. Steady for the grade.

10 ? .... ?

11 Sika 'n' Destroy .... ?
Still no grade known! Has it ever been done?

12 Dret de cuixa .... 7c+

Pa d'alga (7b) on Can Simiro at Arbolí. *Opposite*. Photo: Pete O'Donovan

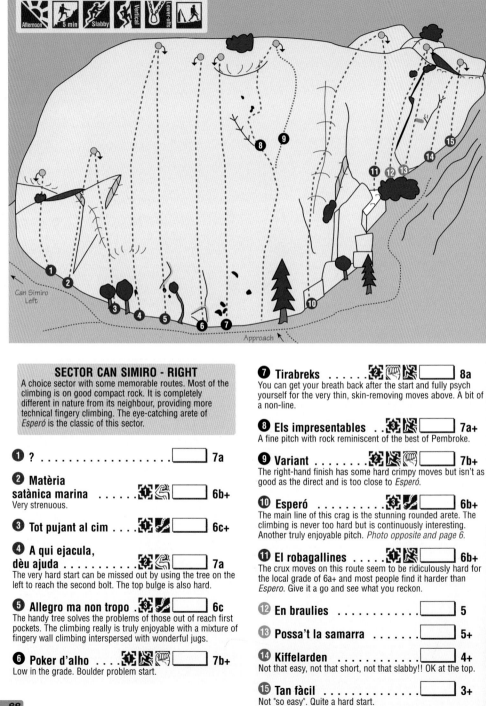

La Mussarra

Mont-ral

Arbolí

Siurana

Montsant

Vilanova de Prades

La Riba

Cogullons

Margalef

SECTOR CAN SIMIRO - RIGHT

A choice sector with some memorable routes. Most of the climbing is on good compact rock. It is completely different in nature from its neighbour, providing more technical fingery climbing. The eye-catching arete of *Esperó* is the classic of this sector.

❶ ? 7a

❷ Matèria satànica marina ...... 6b+
Very strenuous.

❸ Tot pujant al cim .... 6c+

❹ A qui ejacula, dèu ajuda 7a
The very hard start can be missed out by using the tree on the left to reach the second bolt. The top bulge is also hard.

❺ Allegro ma non tropo . 6c
The handy tree solves the problems of those out of reach first pockets. The climbing really is truly enjoyable with a mixture of fingery wall climbing interspersed with wonderful jugs.

❻ Poker d'alho .... 7b+
Low in the grade. Boulder problem start.

❼ Tirabreks 8a
You can get your breath back after the start and fully psych yourself for the very thin, skin-removing moves above. A bit of a non-line.

❽ Els impresentables .. 7a+
A fine pitch with rock reminiscent of the best of Pembroke.

❾ Variant .... 7b+
The right-hand finish has some hard crimpy moves but isn't as good as the direct and is too close to *Esperó*.

❿ Esperó .... 6b+
The main line of this crag is the stunning rounded arete. The climbing is never too hard but is continuously interesting. Another truly enjoyable pitch. *Photo opposite and page 6.*

⓫ El robagallines ..... 6b+
The crux moves on this route seem to be ridiculously hard for the local grade of 6a+ and most people find it harder than *Espero*. Give it a go and see what you reckon.

⓬ En braulies 5

⓭ Possa't la samarra ...... 5+

⓮ Kiffelarden .... 4+
Not that easy, not that short, not that slabby!! OK at the top.

⓯ Tan fàcil .... 3+
Not "so easy". Quite a hard start.

La Mussarra

Mont-ral

Arboli

Siurana

Montsant

Vilanova de Prades

La Riba

Cogullons

Margalef

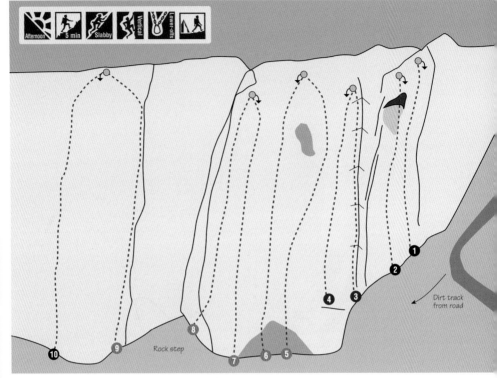

SECTOR EL DUC
The small sector gives some pleasant easier grade climbs on good slabby rock.

APPROACH
From the first parking spot follow a dirt track down hill until the crag appears on the right.

❶ Kiff mi kiwi . . . 8a
This looks good but is hediously thin.

❷ El té cha está . . . 7b
A boulder problem start and a pumpy finish.

❸ Malvasia 7a
A series of bulges with small holds and good rock. A good route.

❹ El handicapat 6c
A strenuous start up the steep flake crack leads to easier climbing above.

❺ Entre pitus i flautes 6a
Climb rightwards over slabby bulges.

❻ Pensaments . . . . 5+
Some steep moves on good holds.

❼ Bola de drap 5
The easiest route here.

❽ Truita en suc 5
Straightforward climbing on good holds.

❾ Ets un Hilary . . . . 5+
Pleasant climbing up the crack.

❿ Mariline . . . . (7a?)
Some doubtful flakes.

EL FALCO

Big pitches, a wonderful setting and stunning views all go together to make El Falco one of the best crags in the Sierra de Prades. Although the number of routes is quite small, all are of quality and are often 45m long. The climbing is very sustained on predominantly vertical or gently impending walls and you will definitely feel that you have put in a good day here if you clock up half a dozen pitches.

Most of the routes are in the 6c to 7b+ categories but are quite reasonable for the grades, being sustained rather than intensely technical or bouldery. All the routes are well bolted but occasionally are a little run-out due to the length of the pitches and the necessity to reduce rope drag.

Equally as good as the climbing is the view across the valley to Siurana, Montsant and beyond. El Falco is rarely busy and can be a good place to get away from people. If you are there on your own, take a moment to listen to the silence.

APPROACH

From the centre of Arbolí village, follow the road south west towards the crags for 1.6km and take a right up a steep tarmac track/road. If approaching from the Roadside Crags then the turn off is about 500m towards Arbolí village from the parking below Can Simiro. After some steep hairpins (750m) a dirt track breaks off to the left on a sharp bend. Go down this dirt track and drive with care as it is narrow, bumpy and muddy at times. After 500m there are small pull-offs for parking in a prominent dip, just following a steep downhill section. From the parking in the dip take the footpath which leads downhill through trees towards the crag. This will take you all of 2 minutes to walk.

ACCESS

Please park with extreme care ensuring you do not block the track in any way as this is used for other traffic. If these parking spots are full there are pull-offs back towards the road. It will add only 5 minutes to your approach.

A WORD ON SAFETY

A 60 metre rope WILL NOT get you anywhere near the ground from many of the lower-offs. Intermediate anchors are in place on the routes where it is necessary but take care on all the long pitches.

LOCAL GUIDEBOOK

A full list of the routes is available in the local guide. See page 6 for details.

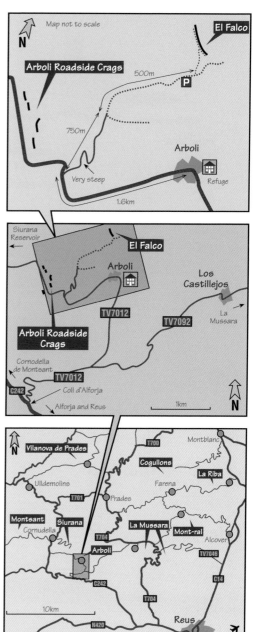

La Mussarra

Mont-ral

Arbolí

Siurana

Montsant

Vilanova de Prades

La Riba

Cogullons

Margalef

EL FALCO - RIGHT

The right-hand side of this fine face has more features than further left but the difficulty level of the better routes is high.

1 Espavila fidel . . . . [ ] **6b**
Short but with some technical slabby moves.

2 De que vas? . . . . [ ] **6a+**
Head into the corner crack to make this an easy route.

3 Que tendre el nezro . . . . . [ ] **6b+**
Has a loose flake.

4 El asesino es el sherif . . [ ] **7b**
A very bouldery route.

5 El tronic . . . . [ ] **8a**

6 Sofa i vidiu . . . . . . [ ] **7b+**
Athletic and pumpy climbing.

7 Jinga . . . . [ ] **7b**
Fine climbing up the orange wall. Never too technical but gives a good forearm pump. A steeper route than other Falco routes.

8 Viros . . . . [ ] **7c+**

9 Fandango . . . . . . [ ] **7b**
The stunning open groove in the perfect grey rock gives a route of superb quality.

10 Tu pa los pollos moreno . . . . . [ ] **7b**
An extremely thin start (tricky first click - use a stick) gives way to some pleasant climbing before entering the final steepening of the corner groove. Great layback moves lead up this to the anchors. *Photo opposite*.

Craig Smith on the upper section of *Tu pa los pollos moreno* (7b) El Falco, Arbolí. *Opposite.* Photo: Alan James

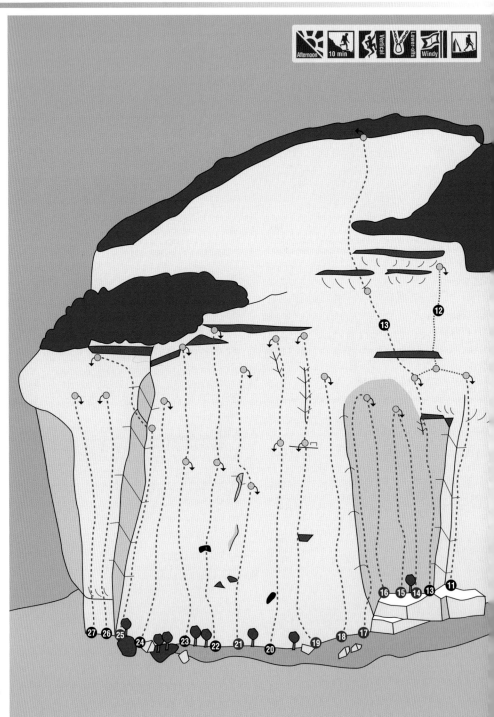

La Mussarra

Mont-ral

Arboli

Siurana

Montsant

Vilanova de Prades

La Riba

Cogullons

Margalef

La Mussarra

Mont-ral

Arboli

Siurana

Montsant

Vilanova de Prades

La Riba

Cogullons

Margalef

The following pitches are all very long and sustained. Some are so long that they have half-height lower-offs although they are usually all climbed as single pitches. **PLEASE TAKE GREAT CARE WHEN LOWERING OFF.**

EL FALCO - LEFT
One of the finest single walls of rock in the area which is especially attractive to those who like gently overhanging face climbing. The routes are all long and absorbing giving sustained climbing often for more than 30m.

⑪ Pa ella y pa los guiris 🔳 7a+
The Smith Rock look-a-like leaning corner gives a magnificent pitch of escalating difficulty. Awkward and hard crux section which may not be enjoyed by everyone. *Photo page 83.*

⑫ Animal 7a+
A high extension to either route 11 or route 13.

⑬ Trenca'm els pinyos 7a+
A long route which is usually only done to the first lower-off.
1) 6c+. Technical climbing with intricate moves leads to some go for it climbing on very smooth holds. Easier climbing sees you to the anchors.
2) 7a. Move up left over the overlap.
3) 7a+. Finish at the top of the crag.
Descent - Walk away from the crag (eastwards) following traces of a path. Walk for 200m to a derelict building. Turn right and follow the edge of a plantation to reach the dirt road. Turn right to reach the car parking spot.

⑭ Bolongo 6c+

⑮ Melissa 6b+
A bouldery start past the first two bolts with lovely continuous climbing above which will always have you literally on your toes.

⑯ Pere mata 6b+
Beautiful climbing in the lower half on some lovely crystalline pockets. As the pockets run out and you find yourself left with foot smears and tiny crimps. Excellent, the best of the three on the ledge. *Photo page 81.*

⑰ Arri ricardo 6c+
32m. The holds never seem too far away as you flow up the steeper lower section. Just as the anchors come into view watch out for the sneaky sting in the tail.

⑱ La miller de 6c
35m. Great climbing from start to finish. Thin moves at the very top are a slight hiccup to the flow of the climbing, just as you thought it was in the bag.

⑲ Haber pedido muerte 6b+
35m. A never-ending pitch. The first half up the rounded orange rock, to the intermediate lower-off, includes the crux.

⑳ Per tutatis 7a+
40m. A memorable pitch perhaps one of the best for the grade in the guidebook. Very long and totally satisfying. 7a to first lower-off. *Photo pages 3 and 31.*

㉑ Borinot 7a
45m to the top. A magnificent pitch of escalating difficulty. The first 20m to the intermediate lower-off gives a good 6b pitch in its own right.

㉒ Chanidangersch 7a+
45m. Another tremendous route giving very sustained and varied climbing although a little run-out in places.

㉓ El Cagat 7b
40m. Another strength-sappingly long route with a hard finishing section.

㉔ Excalibur 7c
30m. A technical route.

㉕ Falcon kreks 6c
Traditional climbing up the long corner.
1) 6c. Follow the corner to a belay.
2) 6c. Move out left onto the wall and up to a lower-off.

㉖ El Sortida 7c+

㉗ Bon Noi 8a

SIURANA

La Mussarra

Mont-ral

Arbolí

Siurana

Montsant

Vilanova de Prades

La Riba

Cogullons

Margalef

The Refuge at Siurana. Photo: Pete O'Donovan

Perched high on an isolated promontory, the tiny Moorish village of Siurana has become a Mecca for many sport climbers over the previous decade. Its position, charm and high quality routes make it one of the most popular winter rock climbing destinations in Europe, and yet with the exception of weekends it rarely feels crowded. The area has been a forcing ground for high standard sport routes since the first bolted climbs appeared in the 80s and is still providing the necessary combination of magnificent challenges and a vibrant scene that produces state-of-the-art pitches.

Siurana used to be one of the remoter climbing locations in the area due to the dreadful state of the approach road that wound its way up from the valley floor but the road has now been resurfaced which has made the approach significantly less taxing. For those wanting to spend an extended time here, non-climbing days can easily be whiled away on the ledges, the one bar, or at the perfectly-positioned refuge, all within walking distance of the crags.

THE ROUTES

Huge bulging grey and orange buttresses are what the best of Siurana is about and there are plenty around, although it comes as a surprise to see what has not yet been developed. The most awe inspiring routes are on sectors Campi Qui Pugui and El Pati, the latter being home to Alex Huber's *La Rambla*, one of the World's first 9a pitches.

For teams operating in the 7s and 8s Siurana will keep providing challenges for many weeks but in the grade range of 5 to 6 the choice is more restricted and the best can probably be bagged in a few days before you move on in search of better pickings elsewhere.

Most of the routes described are well equipped however there are a few which should be given a wide birth and most don't have a bolt at your waist when engaged in the crux moves which makes them difficult to dog. Polish is also becoming a problem on some of the more popular pitches.

Mandrágora (7b) on Sector Esperó Primavera on the Siurana Valley crags. *Page 101*. Photo: Highroglyphics

La Mussarra

Mont-ral

Arboli

Siurana

Montsant

Vilanova de Prades

La Riba

Cogullons

Margalef

CONDITIONS

Climbing conditions can be frustrating varying from snow to blistering sun but even in the middle of winter climbing is rarely out of the question. Siurana itself is at an altitude of 700m and is therefore one of the lower crags in the guide. The majority of the sectors described receive a good deal of sunshine and can get very warm but with careful planning shade can be found throughout the day. Except in the heaviest of rain, climbing is always possible on the steepest of the sectors such as Campi Qui Pugui and l'Olla. If the weather turns cold and windy from a northerly direction most of the south-facing Village Crags will be a haven of calm and warmth.

APPROACH

Siurana is best accessed from the small town of Cornudella de Montsant located on the west side of the Sierra de Prades on the C242. To reach Cornudella de Montsant from Reus take the N420 west out of Reus and after 8km turn right to Bourges del Camp on the C242. Follow this for 21km to Cornudella de Montsant, passing over the Coll d'Alforja on the way. On leaving the town of Cornudella de Montsant on the C242 go 800m then turn right, sign posted 'Siurana'. (Do not turn right too early since this road takes you to the reservoir, signposted 'Panta de Siurana', this leads to Arbolí). The paved road now climbs through beautiful scenery passing the Valley Crags parking at 4.8km and terminates at the Siurana Village parking after 8km. **NOTE** - the large parking area is just on the left as the village comes into sight. Do not drive on towards the village as the parking there is very restricted.

LOCAL FACILITIES

There is now a camp site at Siurana which is situated just before the parking area. It has all the facilities.
The refuge in the village has a shower, toilet, topos and a lively night life at, but if you like your sleep it is better to go else-where. There is accommodation available in the village of Siurana and another campsite at Ulldemolins on the C242 (see accommodation section on page 16).
No goods are available at Siurana itself but the bar serves meals, as does the refuge. Cornudella has numerous bars, cafes and shops for food.
For those without transport Cornudella is one hour's walk from Siurana village or a reliable hitch hike.

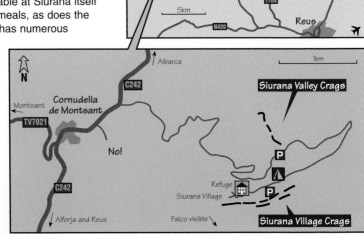

La Mussarra

Mont-ral

Arboli

Siurana

Montsant

Vilanova de Prades

La Riba

Cogullons

Margalef

THE VALLEY CRAGS

The Siurana Valley Crags have some brilliant routes that are often overlooked (in both senses of the word) in favour of the more accessible Village Crags. The small lower-lying valley is ringed by an unbroken line of steep limestone walls undercut by some equally attractive (visually) sandstone cliffs.

Even if you have no time to climb here it is worth a quick look at El Pati sector, home to *La Rambla,* a possible 9a, and a very, very impressive piece of climbing. (A steeper *Cave Route Right-hand* topped off by a chunk of Kilnsey's North Buttress).

APPROACH

All the Valley Crag sectors are approached from the large pullout on the left 4.8kms up the road from the Siurana turn off on the C242, or 3.2km down from the Village Crags car park (pullout on the right). The approach paths are easily located from the pullout.

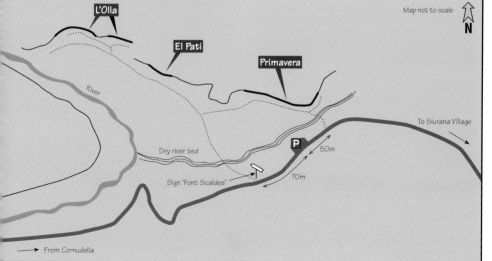

La Mussarra

Mont-ral

Arbolí

Siurana

Montsant

Vilanova de Prades

La Riba

Cogullons

Margalef

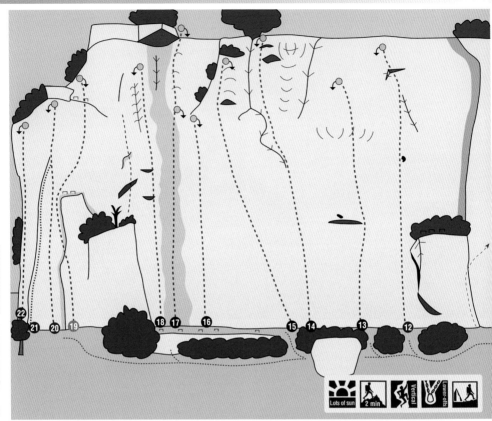

SECTOR ESPERO PRIMAVERA

A fine sector with some long super sustained wall pitches. The sector gets all of the sun that is going and is a great place to warm-up. The sector is easily seen on the approach drive up the valley, especially the prominent orange streak of the classic *Mandragora*.

APPROACH

Walk up the road for 50m and follow a faint path on the left marked by a cairn.

① Records oblidats . . . . . 🔲 6b

1) **6b.** The extreme right-hand line has some good climbing to a belay at 20m.
2) **5.** The corner above to the top.

② Kataplax . . . . 🔲 6c+

A worthwhile pitch giving continually intricate climbing.

③ Pelandruska . . . . 🔲 6b

After a tricky couple of initial moves easier climbing in a great position leads to a belay just to the right of the cave/depression.

④ Esperó primavera . . . 🔲 5+

A superb combination of pitches in a magnificent position with great views down the Siurana Valley.
1) **5+.** From the belay bolt on the ledge climb leftwards up the large flake to clip the first bolt. Continue upwards on superb crinkly rock. After the fifth bolt, trend leftwards to the shared belay at the left side of the cave/depression.
2) **5+.** Move left from the belay and follow a slight weakness up the impressive and exposed wall above to the lower-off.

⑤ Berberechin fibrao . . . . . . 🔲 6b+

A one-move-wonder. One of the hangers is missing making it a touch run-out, although this is on easy ground.

⑥ Ferralladura . . . . 🔲 5+

A good alternative first pitch to start *Esperó Primavera*.

⑦ Penitenciagite . . . 🔲 6b

Some tricky climbing will be encountered on this route if you stick religiously to the line. Most of the difficult bits unfortunately are avoidable.

⑧ El menjapindula . . . . 🔲 7b

A long pitch finishing at the lower-off of the top pitch of *Esperó primavera*.

Left-hand sector

Raised ledge

Small people

Leaning block

Approach

WATCH OUT 5M DROP!

La Mussarra

Mont-ral

Arbolí

Siurana

Montsant

Vilanova de Prades

La Riba

Cogullons

Margalef

⑨ Se miapaga la baldufa . . 🔳 7a
Move right out of *Sayonara Baby* to a mid height lower-off.

⑩ Sayonara Baby . . . 🔳 7b+
The obvious 'v' shaped corner with an extremely steep exit.

⑪ Tan san fot . . . . 🔳 6b
A real delight. Make your way up the chimney and when you can see no more bolts above, move right across the face. There is never anything hard, but the sideways climbing always has you thinking and is very absorbing.

⑫ Remena nena . 🔳 7a+
Excellent wall climbing which is very sustained. As you near the bulge above, you somehow know the crux is waiting for you. Some may find it stretchy, but keep your eyes peeled because there are some good edges to help shorten the gap. Once the bulge is dispensed with, you are almost at the anchors, but there is still a bit more work to do.

⑬ Invierno nuclear . . . . 🔳 7c

⑭ Nola nom . . . . 🔳 7c

⑮ ?

⑯ La via de l'alzina . . . . 🔳 8b

⑰ Mandrágora . . . . 🔳 7b
35m. One of Siurana's classic routes which follows the fine orange streak. It is a little polished around the crux at 10m and is also a bit run-out at this point. There is a mid-height lower-off. *Photo on page 97.*

⑱ Papagora . . . . 🔳 7c
A fine looking line with a bouldery crux.

The next routes start 10m to the left of *Mandragora*.

⑲ Marieta de l'ull viu . . . . 🔳 6a+
Climb up the initial flake and step left onto a ledge. Then comes the short crux. Continue more easily to the top.

⑳ Lamparós toca el dos . 🔳 6b+
The lower moves are really good and make you think. You can get your breath back before the crux and then easy climbing takes you to the anchors. A good pitch.

㉑ Volta i volta . . . . . . 🔳 6b+
The thin crack is a lot harder than it looks with long and sustained moves. This can leave you a bit breathless if you don't hit the sequence right first go.

㉒ Pepitu va de curt . . . . . . 🔳 6c+
The left-hand arete.

La Mussarra

Mont-ral

Arbolí

Siurana

Montsant

Vilanova de Prades

La Riba

Cogullons

Margalef

SECTOR EL PATI

There is not a lot here for the average performer but it is well worth a neck-straining look on your way to Sector L'Olla, or just on a pleasant stroll from the parking. This is certainly the home of the most impressive line in the area, namely *La Rambla,* a possible candidate for 9a.

APPROACH

From the parking area, walk down the road for 70m and take the path on the right. This leads to the wall in 5 minutes.

❶ La Rambla . . . . 🔲 **9a**
A formidable line taking the desperate crack and leaning headwall.

❷ Project . . . . 🔲
A proposed grade of 8c+ has already been offered.

❸ Project . . . . 🔲

❹ Broadway 🔲 **8c+**
Start up *La Rambla.*

❺ La Boqueria . . . 🔲 **8a+**
A fine pitch just to the left of the *La Rambla* headwall.

❻ Esquirol Free . . . 🔲 **7b+**
The trad corner leads to a lower-off below the roof.

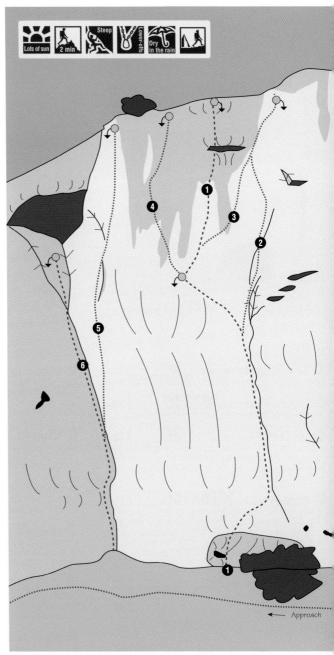

Approach

Steve Dunning on *Migranya* (8b) on Sector L'Olla at Siurana. *Page 105.* Photo: Pete Chadwick

La Mussarra

Mont-ral

Arboli

Siurana

Montsant

Vilanova de Prades

La Riba

Cogullons

Margalef

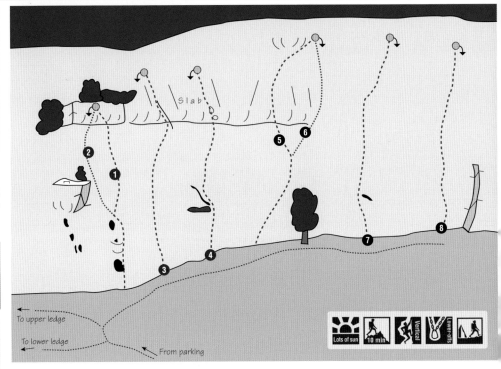

SECTOR L'OLLA - RIGHT
A small but power-packed sector peppered with some tough routes. The right-hand side has a number of intricate and fingery pitches suited to the technician.

❶ **El caganer** 6b
A good warm-up for this crag with a strange line of zig-zagging bolts.

❷ **Cap rapat** 6c
Breaking out left of *El caganer* gives good climbing, joining again with *El caganer* to lower-off.

❸ **Mayling** 6c
An enjoyable climb with a contrasting finalé.

❹ **Guate aquí hay tomate.** 7a
Some steep wall climbing past a move which you may think is the crux, will leave you at the final bulge ..... and the crux! A good route.

❺ **A grasso modo** . . 7b+
The left-hand branch.

❻ **A grosso modo** . . 7b
The right-hand branch.

❼ **Tagediebe** 7c
Staple bolts.

❽ **Echo** 7c

SECTOR L'OLLA - LEFT

The left-hand sector features some perfect tufa trunks tilted at an extremely overhanging angle.

9 Burden chuchen . . . . 🔲 **6c**
A short but steady introductory route to this sector.

10 Nunca me llama mi novia . . 🔲 **6c+**
A difficult first half on monos leads to steeper but easier climbing above. Starting to get harder.

11 Cargol treu banya . . . 🔲 **7a**
A nasty second clip and a bouldery start.

12 Valga'm deu quin patir . . . . 🔲 **7a+**
A long sustained wall climb up the leaning orange wall.

13 Alef Thau . . . . . 🔲 **7b+**
Another good wall climb. A bit run-out and with a one bolt lower-off.

14 Bistec de biceps . . . . 🔲 **7b+**
The first (and easiest) of the amazing steep power routes on this sector. Good holds all the way with a technical wall to finish.

15 Ya os vale . . . . . . 🔲 **7c**
The line of good pockets.

16 Tic i toc . . . . . 🔲 **8a+**
A suspicious looking set of pockets.

17 La cara que no miente 🔲 **8a+**
A magnificent trip up the aesthetic tufa. An iron grip is essential on this one.

18 Patitas de canario 🔲 **8a+**
Link routes on either side.

19 Pota d'elefant . . . . . . 🔲 **7c+**
Start up the elephant's trunk but after a couple of moves head off right up the right-hand flutings to finish on the slab above. Superb moves and recently downgraded.

20 Kurfil . . . . . 🔲 **8a+**
A line of pockets.

21 A cara perro . . 🔲 **8a+**

22 Project . . . . 🔲

23 Umpah pah . . 🔲 **8b**
Fine climbing up the grey streak.

24 Cop de cigala . 🔲 **8a+**
More of the same.

The last two routes start from a higher ledge, below an overhanging flake.

25 Peixa . . . . 🔲 **7c+**
Climb up to a flake and head straight for the top.

26 Migranya . . . . 🔲 **8b**
An amazing climb. From the overhanging flake on the previous route launch out left up the unlikely 5m of leaning wall above.
Photo page 103.

La Mussarra

Mont-ral

Arbolí

Siurana

Montsant

Vilanova de Prades

La Riba

Cogulons

Margalef

Photo: Highroglyphics

VILLAGE CRAGS
Most first experiences of Siurana will be had on the array of sectors located all around the promontory that supports the old village of Siurana itself. Perfectly positioned and having convenient access, these crags are very popular with the Spanish, other Euro-craggers and those from further afield. Nevertheless, turn up mid-week, stroll for five minutes and you will probably be on your own or at worst in the company of one or two other teams. The grade spectrum and pedigree of the routes could not be greater, spanning the gap between one-bolt wonders and world class.

APPROACH
The Village crags are approached from the Siurana village car park 8km from the Siurana turn off on the C242. The sectors are reached (except Reserve India) along a network of ledges and paths that leave the car park at its south east corner and initially run beneath Sector Can melafots.

It is worth paying close attention to the approach map below, and the two alternative descriptions opposite, as some of the path junctions are not easy to spot and require a bit of scrambling to get between rock bands (nothing serious). All of the sectors can be accessed in less than 15 minutes.

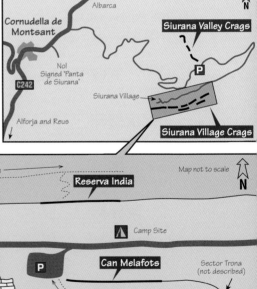

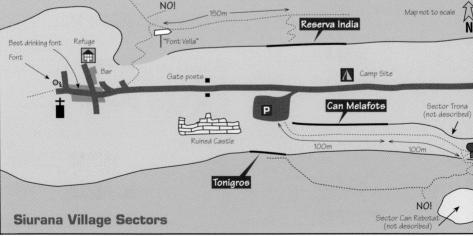

La Mussarra

Mont-ral

Arbolí

Siurana

Montsant

Vilanova de Prades

La Riba

Cogullons

Margalef

APPROACH 1

This approach is shorter for most crags but more difficult to locate.

From the car park walk under **Sector Can Melafots**. 100m past the end of Can Melafots, just after a left-hand bend in the path, is a small cairn and tree on the right. These are opposite the huge pinnacle of Can Rebotat. Facing outwards, scramble carefully back right down ledges and steps to a path at a col. Follow the path leftwards (facing out) down the gully to the left of the huge pinnacle. Stay close to the cliff until you find another path breaking off left to the base of **Sector Can Gan Dionis**. For the other sectors continue descending the gully past a couple of tricky sections. Where the path levels off, head left (do not continue all the way to the river). Keep going along here (some jungle bashing) until **Sector Ca La Boja** appears up and left (recognisable by its roped catwalk up and left of a cave filled with orange bricks). To reach **Sector Campi Qui Pugui** continue on the main path, staying close to the cliff, until a short scramble leads up to the left-hand side of a big bulging wall.

Sector Tonigros - from the path at the col below the cairn and tree, head right (facing out) at first steeply then levelling out until after 200m the sector appears on the right.

APPROACH 2

This approach is longer for most crags but easier to locate and with some great views.

From the car park walk under **Sector Can Melafots**. Continue for about 500m until the path starts to zig-zag downwards below **Sector Can Marges Upper** on the left. The path continues to drop down beneath **Sector Can Marges Lower** on the right. Check the topo on page 112 to locate the scramble up ledges and a short rock gully to the base of **Sector Campi Qui Pugui**. Follow the path under this vast cliff and on into the bushes at its left-hand end. Staying close to the cliff, **Sector Ca La Boja** soon appears on the right (recognisable by its roped catwalk up and left of a cave filled with orange bricks). Continue along the main path and follow it up a gully to the right of a huge pinnacle. After a few tricky sections a path breaks off right beneath **Sector Can Gan Dionis**. The main path continues to a col and then a futher scramble up ledges to the cliff-top path.

Sector Reserva India - From the main parking area walk towards the village. Just before the village drop down a path on the right and follow this for 100m or so until another path appears on the right (signed 'Font Vella'). 150m down here a steep scramble up right gains the cliff base.

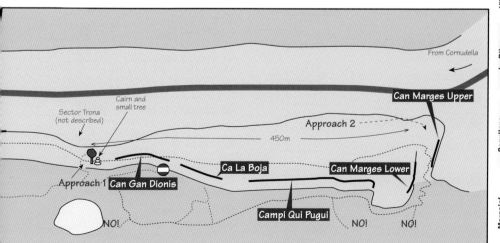

SECTOR CAN MELAFOTS

The uninspiring Sector Can Melafots starts with a series of one and two bolt micro-routes and then rises to a slightly more respectable height. It is of course disproportionately popular since it is only 5 seconds from the car park. Despite this the views are stunning, the early morning temperatures perfect and some of the climbs are better than first appearance might suggest. For the keen leader with a lazy partner this could be the perfect venue as it is possible to belay from your bivi bag.

The first 16 routes of this sector are of minor importance but the odd route is still being squeezed in and throws all the numbering out. It is best to locate the obvious grey streak of route 21 and to work around this.

1 Aresta rucks .... 5+
No gear.

2 Per que triumfi la canalla .. 6b+
Face to right of arete.

3 Escroto roto 6b

4 El paté també te té 7a

5 Tan pa te el té com el paté .. 6c

6 Todo es de color 6c
Obvious corner.

7 Rompe techos .... 6b+

8 Mi primer spit .... 6b+
Lay-back through roof.

9 La rebutosa 7c
Levitate through the bulge.

10 .... 7c+

11 El bocadillitos 7b
Obvious desperate roof crack.

12 Ya cállate .... 6c+

13 Strikomaniac .... 6c+

14 Ya ríete .... 6b+

The crag now increases in height.

15 Bocs de mocs .... 6c+

16 Blancanitos
y los 7 nanieves .... 7a+

17 Garbatx Despistax .... 6c+
If there is a route worth doing on this sector, then this is it. The climbing is sustained and tricky with some final reachy moves just before the anchors.

18 Rémulo y Romo 7a
The first 4m provides a stretchy crux.

19 Cop de só .... 6c+

20 May thing song
ales zinc and punk 7a
A steep finish proves to be very frustrating.

21 Hermano bebe
que la vida es breve ..... 6c+
A good climb taking the grey streak.

22 Trigonometeria . . . . . 🔲🔲⬜ 6a+
One of the longer pitches on a more defined line than others hereabouts.

23 Barrufet . . . . 🔲🔲⬜ 5+
A good start to the day.

24 Gargamel . . . . 🔲⬜ 6a
If you've done the one to the left, then do this too.

25 Mamá ya he spitado . . . . 🔲⬜ 6a+
Start up crack. Climb to the left of a bush and up to a steep finish.

26 Triángulo . . . . 🔲⬜ 5+
A good starter.

27 Llobato . . . . 🔲⬜ 5+

28 Yu vea . . . . 🔲⬜ 6a+
A good climb which can be a bit confusing at the triangular overlap.

29 Viernes 13 . . . . 🔲⬜ 6a+
Similar to the previous route, however the right-hand finish is easier and more obvious.

30 Gat reggae . . . . 🔲⬜ 6c
Some tricky clips and a hard start. Good position.

The next set of routes give probably the best climbing on Can Melafots but they are all hard.

31 Hybrydy, the Future 🔲🔲🔲⬜ 7b+
Low crux move.

32 Der palo torete . . . . 🔲⬜ 7c

33 Bestiola . . . . . . 🔲🔲🔲⬜ 8a+

34 Punyatera . . . . . 🔲🔲🔲⬜ 8a

35 Hòstia . . . . 🔲🔲🔲⬜ 7b
Photo on page 111.

36 Tu no can melafots, bou . 🔲⬜ 7b+

37 Pizza de pinya . . . . . 🔲🔲⬜ 7a
The best route on the sector. A bouldery start leads to a reachy mid section followed by a juggy finale.

La Mussarra

Mont-ral

Arbolí

Siurana

Montsant

Vilanova de Prades

La Riba

Cogullons

Margalef

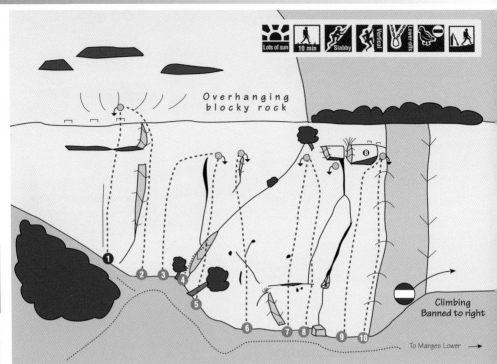

SECTOR CAN MARGES - UPPER

The Can Marges sectors consist of two contrasting chunks of limestone. The Upper Sector provides some pleasant easier pitches, on excellent rock, which require good technique and little pulling power.

There is a climbing restriction due to birds on the right-hand end of the crag.

APPROACH - use Approach 1 on page 106

From Sector Can Melafots walk along the main ledge path for 500m until it zig-zags downhill below Can Marges Upper on the left.

❶ Re i no re més 6c
The gear on this route is in a terrible state. Leave well alone.

❷ Passatemps 6a
Very bad gear, especially at the lower-off.

❸ Escuela de calor 6a
Bizarre. No lower-off of its own.

❹ Fletxa 5
Start by the tree and climb a crack directly to the lower-off.

❺ Fletxa directa . . . . . 5+
Start down and right and climb straight up to the crack of the original line. Fingery.

❻ Spit de boira . . . . 5+
High step-ups leave you at a heart-fluttery distance above the bolts. Very worthwhile.

❼ Última del 85 . . . 6a
A fairly steep start with good pockets on the wall above. Be careful at the second clip. Bolted with staples.

❽ Cos lo cao . . . . 5+
More good climbing. Start left of the wide right-slanting crack. Climb up to the thin crack and continue directly up the wall above to the lower-off on *Ultima del 85*.

❾ La osa golosa . . . . 5+
Very enjoyable climbing starting just right of a slanting crack.

❿ Cos que cao 6a
Steep start with slabbier finish. Bolted with staples.

⛔ No Climbing to the right of this route because of bird restriction (all year ban).

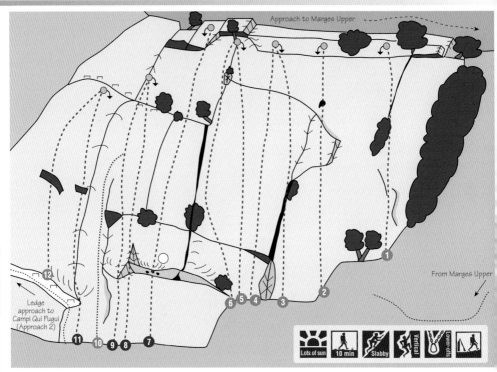

SECTOR CAN MARGES - LOWER

The rock is excellent and the crack lines on the right of the crag provide some very nice climbing at amenable grades. Further left are some longer pitches with butch starts.

APPROACH - use Approach 1 on page 106

From Sector Can Melafots walk along the main ledge path for 500m until it zig-zags downhill below Can Marges Upper on the left. The Lower Sector is 20m further down the path on the right.

❶ ? **5**
The first route is as good as any to start with before you tick the crag.

❷ Currupipi **5**
Climb the slabby start, over the flake and continue up the thin crack to the top.

❸ Ay candemor **5**
Start right of the crack. Cross over it and continue to the top.

❹ Can fanga . . . . **5+**
Start left of the wide crack. Very nice.

❺ Trimegesto . . . . **5+**
Nice climbing on water pockets and dimples. Poor first bolt. *Photo opposite.*

❻ Jota negra . . . . **5+**
Head left for the crack and follow it to the top.

The next routes are a bit longer and have some steep starts.

❼ Calidoscopi **6c**
A steep pull through the starting bulge leads to some lovely wall climbing above.

❽ No dan bolsa . . . . . . **6c+**
Steep moves over the ominous looking bulge.

❾ Esquivapins **6c**
Climb the right-hand side of the corner crack, through bulges to lower-off above the ledge.

❿ Pixapins . . . . **6a+**
Climb the left-hand side of the corner and join *Esquivapins*.

⓫ Extremoduro . . . . **6b+**
Start at the bulging arete. Make some stiff pulls through the bulge and continue trending leftwards to lower-off.

⓬ Tahona . . . . **5+**
Start from the raised ledge on the left and climb the crinkled wall above with an overlap at half height.

Emma Medara on *Trimegesto* (5+) on Sector Can Marges Upper at Siurana. *Opposite.* Photo: Highroglyphics

Anabolica (8a) Sector Campi Qui Puigui, Siurana. *Page 116.* Photo: Highroglyphics

SECTOR CAMPI QUI PUGUI

Campi Qui Pugui is one of Spain's most famous cliffs and is the showpiece sector of Siurana. It is jam-packed with around forty sensational pitches, most of which are above 7a+ and, as the difficulty increases, so does the quality. The left-hand side consists of a massive bulging wall with few lines of obvious weakness. The rock is superb and generally gives positive holds and good pockets of all shapes and sizes. All the routes are well equipped.

PROJECTS
It is worth bearing in mind that projects spring up on this wall quite regularly so check at the refuge if in doubt.

APPROACH - see map on page 106
APPROACH 1 - From the car park walk under Sector Can Melafots. 100m past the end of Can Melafots, just after a left-hand bend in the path, is a small cairn and tree on the right. These are opposite the huge pinnacle of Can Rebotat. Facing outwards, scramble carefully back right down ledges and steps to a path at a col. Follow the path leftwards (facing out) down the gully to the left of the huge pinnacle. Stay close to the cliff until you find another path breaking off left to the base of Sector Can Gan Dionis. Continue descending the gully past a couple of tricky sections. Where the path levels off head left (direct goes all the way to the river). Keep going along here (some jungle bashing) until Sector Ca La Boja appears up and left (recognisable by its roped catwalk up and left of a cave filled with orange bricks). To reach Sector Campi Qui Pugui continue on the main path, staying close to the cliff, until a short scramble leads up to the left-hand side of a big bulging wall.

APPROACH 2 - From the car park walk under Sector Can Melafots. Continue for about 500m until the path starts to zig-zag downwards below Sector Can Marges Upper on the left. The path continues to drop down beneath Sector Can Marges Lower on the right. Check the topo on page 112 to locate the scramble up ledges and a short rock gully to the base of Sector Campi Qui Pugui.

RIGHT-HAND SECTOR
The right-hand sector has some excellent routes but is slightly overshadowed by its neighbour.

❶ **Gosgondriol constrictor** . . 🖼️▢ 6b+
A one-move-wonder, with the one move being particularly difficult and with a nasty fall potential.

❷ **Sublim obsessió** . . . . ▢ 7c+
A difficult pitch tucked away in the corner near the toilet.

The next eight routes start from the narrow ledge easily accessed from the large gaping cavern.

❸ **Tros de ruc** . . . . 🔣▢ 7b+
Difficult climbing up the leaning corner groove gives way to the pleasant crack above.

❹ **Terrorisme autoritzat** . . . . 🔣🖼️🖼️▢ 7b+
Some difficult pocket pulling, followed immediately by thin fingery moves deposit you underneath a groove. Once over the bulge, the slab is easier but not a path. High in the grade.

La Mussara

Mont-ral

Arbolí

Siurana

Montsant

Vilanova de Prades

La Riba

Cogullons

Margalef

La Mussarra

Mont-ral

Arbolí

Siurana

Montsant

Vilanova de Prades

La Riba

Cogullons

Margalef

⑤ Rodríguez & Rodríguez 7b+
A prominent line on this section which is continuous and good.

⑥ Cañilla ris pal sobre 7c

⑦ Frodo nuevededos . . . 7a+
Steep cranking up the wall to the right of a pocketed diagonal crack.

The next three routes start from where the ledge narrows to almost nothing so make sure you belay at the bottom. They are all short and bouldery hence the grade seems stiff!

⑧ Maese Samsagaz . . . 7a

⑨ Bisky on the Rocks . . 7a

⑩ Tapbioles I Pirretes . . 6c+

The next routes are accessed from the main path leading around the base of the crag.

⑪ Saiko dase . . . . . 6b+
An old fashioned style route. Start easily and end with difficulty way above the bolt.

⑫ Gamba gamba 7b
Good sustained wall climbing. Watch out for the 4th clip.

⑬ Cruela de ville 7b
Low in the grade with a hardish crux move.

The next 5 routes start on a higher ledge accessed from the left.

⑭ Harry el brut 7b
Starts on the far right-hand end of this ledge and takes the right-hand most-bolted line.

⑮ Tanoka . . . . 7c+
Share the start of *Harry el Brut*.

⑯ Eixuga-me-la i tornem-hi 7c+
Breache the middle of the impressive bulge via a pocket. Above this move things get easier but without much rest.

⑰ Samba pal gringo . 8a+

⑱ El logurin 7a
A good crack climb but with some big lob potential. It might be worth stretching your inner thighs before you start up this one.

The next three routes are accessed from an even higher ledge reached by scrambling up a steep 3m corner which divides the left and right-hand walls of the Campi Qui Pugui sectors.

⑲ Toca-me-la sam . . 6c+
An appealing pitch up the orange wall and well-chalked holds.

⑳ Segueix-me-la tocant . . . 7b+
A top pitch to *Toca-me-la sam*.

㉑ Tasta 7a

S L A B

La Mussarra

Mont-ral

Arbolí

Siurana

Montsant

Vilanova de Prades

La Riba

Cogullons

Margalef

Steep wall

← To Ca La Boja

From right-hand sector

Right-hand sector

CAMPI QUI PUGUI - LEFT

The really world-class climbing is on the awesome left-hand side of this fine wall.

❶ Accelera virtuoso 🔳🔳🔳 8a
One for the strong-fingered.

❷ Isadora dónde estás 🔳🔳🔳 7b
The easiest route on this sector is an appealing line but it is definitely showing the signs of over-use. Excellent nevertheless.

❸ Adria 6a
A continuation pitch to either of the previous two routes.

❹ Siouxie ..... 🔳🔳🔳🔳 7c+
A superb route. The crux is m oving right from the short arete in the middle of the wall.

❺ Project ....

❻ Un rato en cada postura .... 🔳🔳 8a

❼ La balada des pendus 8b

❽ Gigololo .... 🔳🔳 8a+
Start up *Anabólica* before moving out rightwards.

❾ Anabólica ..... 🔳🔳🔳 8a
A magnificent pitch that breaches the most impressive section of this frozen wave of rock. *Photo on page 114.*

❿ Mr. Cheki ..... 🔳🔳🔳 8b+

⓫ Bou I prou .... 🔳🔳 8b

⓬ Project .... (8b)

⓭ El membre ... 🔳🔳🔳🔳 8c

⓮ L'odi social .... 🔳 8c+

⓯ Project ....

⓰ Renegoide .... 🔳🔳 8b+
A very short route.

The next five routes start on a raised ledged accessed by scrambling up the polished wall.

⓱ Gurungos .... 🔳🔳🔳🔳 7b
27m. Not one for the nervous. A bouldery first 6m leads to a rest. The crux crimpy wall comes next then easier and enjoyable climbing to anchors. Often has a wasp's nest.

⓲ Cleptomanía .... 🔳🔳🔳 7c
A brilliant pitch giving mainly fingery wall climbing punctuated by a steep crux bulge. Some bolts are a bit spaced.

⓳ Triste pesadilla 🔳🔳🔳🔳 7b+
A cracking pitch with some bulging sections, very technical moves and a tough sprint for the anchor.

⓴ Lullaby .... 🔳🔳🔳 7c
Follow the attractive blue/grey streak. An intense one-move wonder.

㉑ Delicatessen ..... 🔳🔳 7a+
A brilliant overhanging face with good pockets and crimps. The bolts are in strange places.

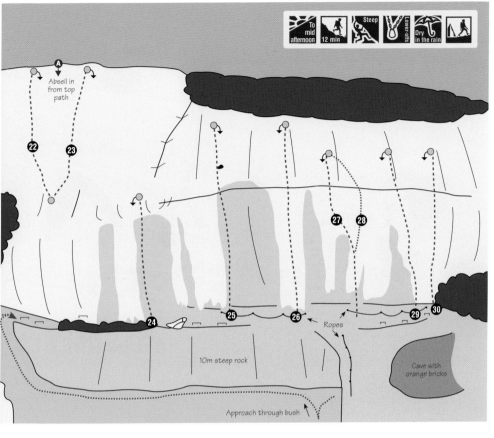

La Mussarra

Mont-ral

Arboli

Siurana

Montsant

Vilanova de Prades

La Riba

Cogullons

Margalef

SECTOR CA LA BOJA

Ca la Boja offers a choice selection of pitches similar in character to those on the adjoining Campi Qui Pugui. This sector gets less attention however due to the belay ledge being about 10m above the ground and none too spacious in places. This ledge is approached from the left-hand side of the crag.

APPROACH - see map and descriptions on page 106

Sector Ca La Boja can be approached by either of the methods on page 106.

The first two routes start from a belay reached via an abseil located on the upper path.

㉒ Trulla Trulla . . . . . . 🔳🔳 ⬜ 7b+

㉓ . . . . 🔳🔳 ⬜ 7b+

㉔ Madame Pompadu 🔳🔳🔳 ⬜ 7b+
Start from the raised ledge below the first line of bolts. Some good pockets to start lead to some trying moves above before the angle eases.

㉕ La loca más loca del bodevil . . . .🔳🔳🔳 ⬜ 7b+
The line follows a stunning bit of rock but it has been hacked about and has one of those moves you'll either love or hate. Cruise up to the move and 'lay one on' for the obvious hold. Being tall may not help much since you have to get your feet very high for the dyno. *Photo on page 7.*

㉖ Fam de Mai . . 🔳🔳🔳🔳 ⬜ 8a+
A beautiful piece of rock. The central grey streak from the right-hand side of the rope hand rail

㉗ Trierer Weg . . 🔳🔳🔳🔳 ⬜ 8a+
The left-hand line of bolts breaking out of *Druuna*.

㉘ Druuna . . . . 🔳🔳 ⬜ 7c+

㉙ L'esferit . . . . 🔳🔳 ⬜ 7b+

㉚ Hook . . . . 🔳🔳 ⬜ 7b
The far right of the wall.

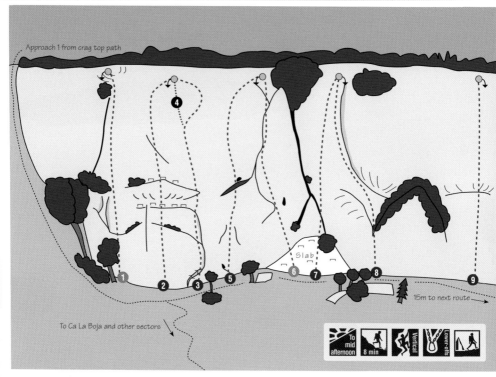

Approach 1 from crag top path

Slab

15m to next route

To Ca La Boja and other sectors

To mid afternoon | 8 min | Vertical | Lower-offs

La Mussarra

Mont-ral

Arbolí

Siurana

Montsant

Vilanova de Prades

La Riba

Cogullons

Margalef

SECTOR CAN GAN DIONIS - LEFT

A fine sector with some quality pitches which are much longer than they appear. The vertical rock gives technical climbing and the grades can seem hard for those used to steeper ground.

APPROACH - see map on page 106 (Approach 1)

From the car park walk under Sector Can Melafots. 100m past the end of Can Melafots, just after a left-hand bend in the path, is a small cairn and tree on the right. These are opposite the huge pinnacle of Can Rebotat. Facing outwards, scramble carefully back right down ledges and steps to a path at a col. Follow the path leftwards (facing out) down the gully to the left of the huge pinnacle. Stay close to the cliff until you find another path breaking off left to the base of Sector Can Gan Dionis.

① Tubergolosa . . . . 5+

A good warm-up route but bear in mind that all these routes are pretty stout for the grade.

② Escaralamoza 6c

Very good climbing up the steep wall with wicked crux moves.

③ Eto e tota 6c

The fine central line. Where the 7b variant heads straight up, make sure you pick the right line. Odd bolts.

④ Eto e má 7b

A variation finish to *Eto e tota*. Head straight up at the second to last bolt.

⑤ Esconderos agujidos . . . . 6c+

A very sustained bit of climbing. An especially difficult start past some thin seams and a tricky finish.

⑥ Eto e diferente 6a

Enjoyable climbing up the curving flake crack.

⑦ Pimientos en pepitoria . . 6b

⑧ Hielo gris 6b

An atypical route for Siurana and a much needed rest from the tendon-twanging pocket-pulling hereabouts. Very good.

⑨ Chute de jalea . . . . . 6c+

Bulging rock

NO ACCESS TO
CA LA BOJA

La Mussarra

Mont-ral

Arboli

Siurana

Montsant

Vilanova de Prades

La Riba

Cogullons

Margalef

SECTOR CAN GAN DIONIS - RIGHT
The right-hand end of this crag has some more quality technical routes. The classic groove line of *Massa temps sense piano* is the main attraction, the surrounding routes are nearly as good.

⑩ Agonías . . . . 6c+
The start of this route is 15m from *Chute de jalea* and just as the path begins to drop down hill.

⑪ No tires tanto que te pones tonto 7a
An appalling route which sums up the worst of Siurana - chipped and drilled to someone's own personal dimensions. Start at a gap in the bushes, if you really want to.

⑫ L'imperi dels sentits . . . . 7b+
To start scramble up leftwards through bushes to a ledge.

⑬ S'ha de badar . 7a+
Originally graded 7a, this sustained and technical wall climb definitely deserves its upgrading. Rock-over technicians will be in their element. Start up *Massa temps sense piano* to the 1st bolt.

⑭ Massa temps sense piano 6c
A brilliant line giving sustained and difficult climbing. Originally 6b+, it is now regraded more realistically although bolts desperately need replacing.

⑮ Il n'ya pas de quoi . 7c

⑯ Prendre la tête . . 7a+
A well positioned route. The high first bolt is easy to reach.

⑰ Kurt de gandals . . 7b+
Short and fierce. Ground fall potential clipping the first bolt. The name is painted on the rock.

⑱ Dios nidor . . . 7c+
A fine route but Mr. Drill has been to work on 2 finger pockets. The name is painted on the rock.

⑲ Cólico nefritico 6c
Excellent climbing in a great position. Very sustained with great character. Start in the tree.

⑳ No escalfis que és pitjor 7b
It shares its start with *Colico nefritico*.

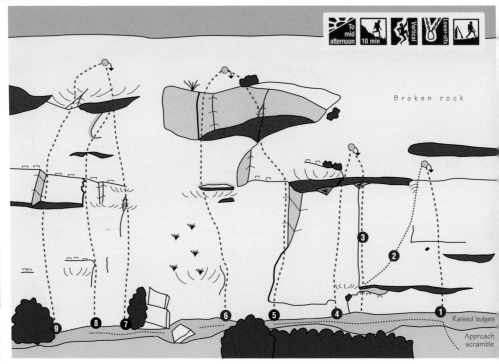

La Mussara

Mont-ral

Arboli

Siurana

Montsant

Vilanova de Prades

La Riba

Cogullons

Margalef

SECTOR TONIGROS

Sector Tonigros is one of the warmest spots at Siurana since it is sheltered and south facing. A handful of longish routes will give a good day's sport or is useful as an end-of-day venue for a quick couple of ticks. The sector is directly below the car park.

APPROACH - see map on page 106 (Approach 1)

From the car park walk under Sector Can Melafots. 100m past the end of Can Melafots, just after a left-hand bend in the path, is a small cairn and tree on the right. These are opposite the huge pinnacle of Can Rebotat. Facing outwards, scramble carefully back right down ledges and steps to a path at a col. Head right (facing out) at first steeply then levelling out until after 200m the sector appears on the right.

❶ Putuliken . . . . . . 🔲🔲🔲 **6c+**

❷ La fura dels baus . . . 🔲🔲 **6c**
The rock is very good and pocketed and the climbing is sustained for such a short route.

❸ Poll remullat . . . . 🔲 **6b+**
The thin crack. The best of the four shorter routes.

❹ Estrany parany . . . . . . 🔲🔲 **6b**
The first wall is pretty tame but higher up it gets exciting when you start swinging wildly around the bulge. (You may of course find a better way to do it).

❺ Petit pro eixerit . . . 🔲🔲🔲 **7a+**
Perhaps the worst climb on this sector. It wanders around and only has one bit of good climbing on the pocketed wall high up. Be careful because the bolt on the lip of the roof is badly placed.

❻ Antaviana . . . . 🔲 **6c+**

❼ Black uhuru . . 🔲🔲🔲🔲 **7b**

❽ Humor de gos . . . 🔲🔲🔲🔲 **7a+**
The hardest is saved to the last and feels a bit run-out if you are of a nervous disposition.

❾ Jugant amb foc . . . . . . 🔲🔲 **7a**
The lower section is enjoyable and fairly steady. Then comes the crux which is only short but with some very prickly holds.

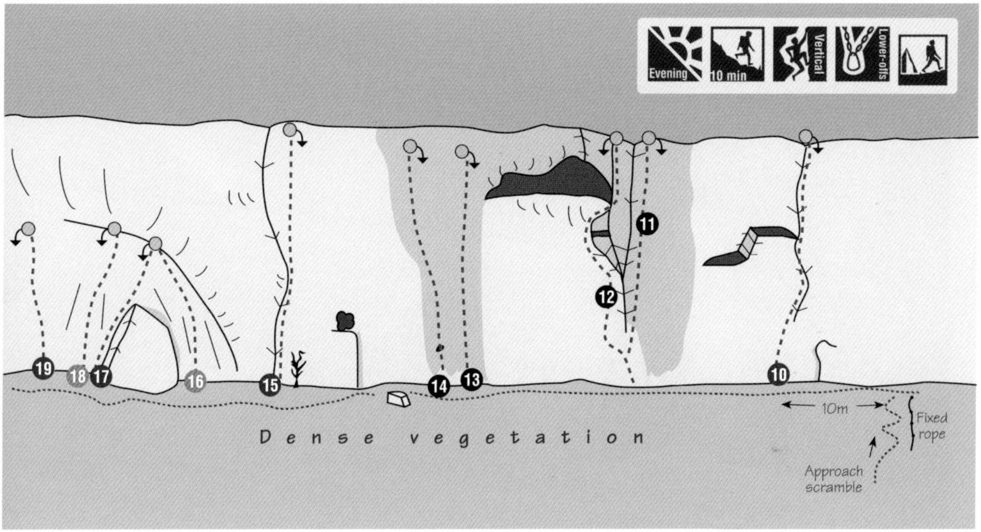

La Mussarra

Mont-ral

Arbolí

Siurana

Montsant

Vilanova de Prades

La Riba

Cogullons

Margalef

SECTOR RESERVA INDIA

This sector is north-facing and is very useful should temperatures become unbearably high elsewhere. There are some great lines and the majority of pitches are long and sustained. The rock quality is a little variable since the routes get less traffic than elsewhere.

APPROACH - see map on page 106

From the main parking area walk towards the village. Just before the village drop down a path on the right and follow this for 100m or so until another path appears on the right (signed 'Font Vella'). 150m down here a steep scramble up right gains the cliff base.

⑩ Jeronimo . . . . 🕱🕱 ☐ 7a
The soaring groove line is extremely appealing and gives sustained and absorbing climbing. The rock is friable in places, especially at the start.

⑪ Cheyene . . . . 🕱🕱 ☐ 7b
Climb the groove to the right of the massive prow. A good line.

⑫ Yanomami . . . . 🕱🕱 ☐ 8a
Break out left from *Cheyene* and head up the wall straight for the impressive crack splitting the left wall of the prow. Another good pitch.

⑬ Vitz platt . . . . . . 🕱🕱🕱 ☐ ?
Start 15m left of *Yanomami*. Take a line of flake holds in the shallow grey groove. Grade lost in the editing.

⑭ No Sika Please . . 🕱🕱🕱 ☐ 7a+
The more obvious groove just of left *Vitz Platt* which soars a long way up the crag.

⑮ Ojo negro . . . . 🕱 ☐ 6b+
Start 15m left of *No Sika Please*. An excellent route following the curving groove. Some very intricate climbing keeps your attention.

⑯ Sioux . . . . 🕱 ☐ 6a+
Start 15m left of *Ojo Negro*. Delicate climbing to the right of the block.

⑰ Cheroki . . . . ☐ 6c
Climb behind the left-hand side of the block.

⑱ Apache . . . . 🕱 ☐ 5+
Nice climbing with a puzzling finish.

⑲ Navajos . . . . . . 🕱🕱🕱 ☐ 6c+
The far left-hand route is for slab masters.

MONTSANT

The amazing Barrots buttress at Montsant. Photo: Alan James

Looking to the west from El Falco, Arbolí or Siurana the unmistakable mountain range of the Sierra de Montsant is a constant attraction to the eye of any climber. It is obvious that the range contains vast cliffs but like so many distant crags, visitors with a limited time never set foot in the range let alone on the climbs. A day or two spent climbing in the one area described in detail here, known as Barrots, will certainly reveal the potential of the area which will undoubtedly become a major destination in the coming years. Approaches are described to four further areas for those who wish to explore a bit.

The routes at Barrots are as good as any in this guidebook and their position is simply awe-inspiring. The generally south-facing, unbroken line of cliffs stretch for miles and, although up to around 200m high, are conveniently split in to tiers linked by spectacular paths and ladders. The *Barrots-Carrasclets* round trip gives a great half-day hike-come-scramble and would make a fun rest day excursion. It is described on the next page.

The geology at Montsant is completely different from that of Siurana and La Mussara and is similar to that at Vilanova de Prades, being tufa-coated conglomerate, but on a much larger scale. This form of conglomerate provides a superb climbing surface which gives the appearance of pocketed limestone.

THE ROUTES

The routes described are all single-pitch and the ground can easily be reached from the lower-offs with a 60m rope. The routes are extremely sustained and most are either gently overhanging or even steeper. The holds are generally good but, being pocketed, footholds have a tendency to disappear from view when looking down.

The terraced nature of the crag guarantees instant exposure on many pitches despite the fact that the dividing ledges are actually quite spacious.

Unfortunately there are no routes below 6b although there is great potential for development at this level and easier. The best way to get a sample of this area would be to pick off a couple of the routes on the lower cliffs before heading for the main ledge higher up. If you can drag yourself away before nightfall it is best to wander back via the *Carrasclets* descent for a totally memorable day out.

CONDITIONS

The cliff line faces due south but a number of the routes will get some shade in the afternoon, however this area is generally warm when the sun is out. The upper ledges are cooler and can be breezy. This is not a good place to be in poor weather since it is at an altitude of over a 1000m and very exposed

APPROACH

From Cornudella de Montsant (approaching from Reus) turn left as soon as you enter Cornudella on the TV-7021, sign posted to 'Morera' 8.5 km. Take this road for 8km to the village of Morera de Montsant. At Morera take the right fork and drive into the village (not the way marked 'Scala Dei') through the narrow streets. At the Place del Priorat turn right then take the second right onto the 'Carrer de la Bassa'. At the end turn left and park in the large parking area.

LOCAL FACILITIES

There are no shopping facilities at Morera de Montsant but there is a font in the square and a restaurant. Cornudella is only 8km away which is the nearest place to pick up provisions. There is no accommodation.

La Mussarra

Mont-ral

Arboli

Siurana

Montsant

Vilanova de Prades

La Riba

Cogullons

Margalef

La Mussarra

Mont-ral

Arboli

Siurana

Montsant

Vilanova de Prades

La Riba

Cogullons

Margalef

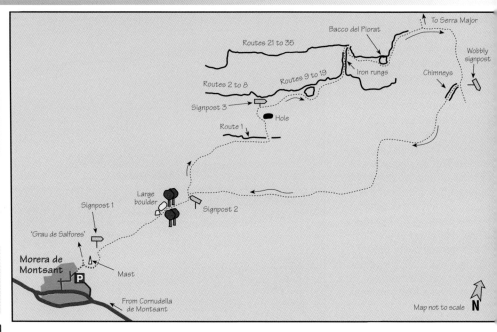

Map not to scale N

THE BARROTS-CARRASCLETS LOOP WALK
This walk is a great outing in itself so even if you don't take your rack to climb at Barrots and just fancy a look, continue around the loop.

NOTE: This is not a walk for non-climbers since the descent at the end is quite difficult.

Follow the approach description to the left to the third signpost. Continue in the direction to Barrots as it heads upwards weaving around the base of the rock buttresses, until you enter the large chimney. Scramble up this and climb up via the iron hand/foot holds. At the top there is climbing on the left-hand side of the ledge. You want to head around the ledge system on the right, crossing the wedged block via the iron holds. The path is obvious as it ventures around the often narrow ledges, marked by red and black paint. Take care on the narrowest points where the ledge has been eroded away. These sections have cable wires to hold on to. The 'Balcony de Priorat' is a great view point. The path continues around the ledge system passing route number 36 and then splits at a signpost. There are paths which will take you over the top of the Serra Major but the Carrasclets path goes on round the ledge system. About 100m past this signpost you'll come to a wobbly one with Carrasclets marked. You will see some old tape heading down and a cable iron rung ladder. This is where you are going. Not the place to go if you've been eating too much paella because you could get wedged. Three sections of chimney will bring you to the footpath again which you follow until it brings you back to signpost number 2.

APPROACH TO THE CLIMBING
The crags are visible from the parking area at the top of the village. You are taking a walkers' footpath to Barrots marked with signs and mainly yellow and white paint (sometimes red/white and sometimes red/black). From the parking take the track west signposted 'Serra Major Barrots'. Follow this as it curves around below the TV mast and heads in an easterly direction. You will soon come to a signpost, follow the direction to Barrots. Eventually you will come to another post. Again follow Barrots direction (if you are doing the Carrasclets circuit you will end up back at this point). The path now heads more steeply uphill and is a bit like walking up a steep pebble beach. The path levels off as you arrive at the terrace below rock walls. Follow the path rightwards and you will come to the first route *First Hand '88*, a poor route. Carry on for the better routes as marked on the overview map, always taking the direction of Barrots.

The magnificent
Route 35 (7a+)
the upper tier
Barrots, Montsant.
page 127.
Photo: Highroglyphics

La Mussarra

Mont-ral

Arbolí

Siurana

Montsant

Vilanova de Prades

La Riba

Cogullons

Margalef

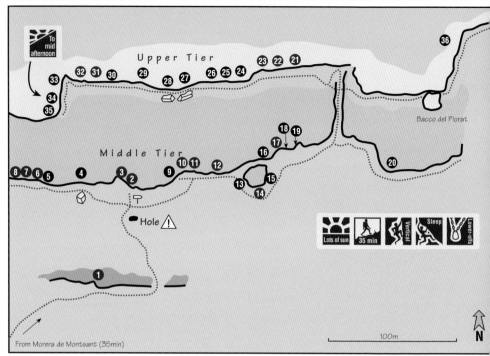

Upper Tier

Middle Tier

Bacco del Piorat

Hole ⚠

Lots of sun | 35 min | Vertical | Steep | Lower-offs

From Morera de Montsant (35min)

100m

N

LOWER TIER

❶ First Hand '88 ...... 🖐️🔀⬜ 6c+
The brutal overhanging thin crack. Walk on by for better climbing.

> **MIDDLE TIER**
> From route 1 follow the path rightwards for 30m then scramble upwards by some black and red markers. At a split in the path head left, passing a deep hole on the right, to reach a signpost. The following routes are straight ahead.

❷ Star in Tokio .... 🔲🔀🔀⬜ 6b+
29m. A long pitch of sustained off-vertical face climbing. Take care when lowering off.

❸ Café con leche
con más café ...... 🔲🔀🔀⬜ 6b+
29m. Similar to *Star in Tokio*.

❹ .... 🔀🔀⬜ 7c?
Start on the block and follow intermittent flared cracks. The rock is a bit crumbly.

❺ .... 🔲🔀⬜ ?
The right-hand of four routes on this small sector.

❻ .... 🔲🔀⬜ 6c
Start to the left of the thin seam.

❼ .... 🔲🔀⬜ 6b+
Sustained wall.

❽ .... 🔲🔀⬜ 6c
Just right of the vegetated crack.

The next two lines are just left of where the path arrives at the cliff.

❾ .... ⬜ ?

❿ .... 🔲🔀⬜ 6b+
Sustained and intricate moves all the way.

⓫ .... 🔲🔀⬜ 6b
The fine twisting groove is a fine pitch with big holds and plenty of bridging. Brilliant. *Photo on page 19.*

12 . . . . **6c+**
Another sustained pocketed wall.

13 . . . . **?**
A line up the west face of the pillar.

14 Hopi **6c**
A nice route up the east face of the pillar. Some friable rock.

15 . . . . **?**
The right-hand line.

16 Parc güell . . . . **7b+**
The steep bulge and rounded arete.

17 Yogi . . . . **6c+**
The wall just left of the corner.

18 Corner . . . . **?**
The obvious corner with the bolts just to the right.

19 . . . . **?**
Wall to the right.

To get to route 20, don't go up the chimney/gully, but continue around the ledge at the same level.

**20 It seems easy
but it's not difficult** . . . . **?**
That really is the route name. Sadly no grade is known at present.

UPPER TIER
The rest of the routes are on the highest level. Scramble up the chimney/gully under the huge chockstone, then up the iron rungs on the right wall. Follow the shelf back left onto a wide ledge below the cliff.

21 Cometa pupazza **6c**
A deceptive and brilliant route. The difficulties increase with height gained so be prepared.

22 . . . . **7a**
This is a really gnarly piece of committing wall work and it will sort out those who thought it looked like a sort touch.

23 The Hole . . . . **6b+**
The easiest route on the ledge gives a good outing.

24 The Rose **7c**
Superb pumpy climbing with the odd tricky move thrown in to keep things interesting.

25 . . . . **7c**
A steep finish lurks above the pumpy lower section.

26 Sagrada familia . . **7c**
Tremendous stamina work once again leaves you gasping below the final wall. The crux is a hideous move on sharp holds.

TAKE GREAT CARE NOT TO DISLODGE ROCKS FROM THE LEDGE BENEATH THE NEXT FEW CLIMBS SINCE THERE MAY WELL BE CLIMBERS AND WALKERS DIRECTLY BELOW.

27 . . . . **7c+**
The crux is pulling through the bulge.

28 . . . . **7c**
Start by the boulders and grapple with this meaty number. Looks like it should be harder.

29 . . . . **7c**
Jugs lead up the grey overhanging streak. Belay/cleaning bolt on mid-route ledge.

The next line of bolts is an unknown new line. Then comes:

30
Three bolts to nowhere.

31 . . . . **7a**
Poor rock.

32 . . . . **6c+**
Poor rock.

33 . . . . **7b**
The first of this magnificent trio is the hardest but perhaps has the best moves. All the clips are next to jugs. Well steep!

34 . . . . **7a+**
Simply wonderful climbing on an unlikely bit of wall but it is best not to look down when clipping as the run-outs are impressive. Only seven bolts.

35 . . . . **7a+**
Fantastic position and a couple of technical bits. Take care on the first 5m as some of the rock is a bit crumbly.
Photo on page 125.

The last route is passed if you continue on the Barrots-Carrascelets walk. Use the iron rungs to cross over to the other side of the chimney and continue for 200m to a small alcove and the bolt line.

36 . . . . **8a?**
A neck-craning line. A 45° leaning wall capped by an awesome roof crack.

La Mussarra

Mont-ral

Arbolí

Siurana

Montsant

Vilanova de Prades

La Riba

Cogullons

Margalef

Left margin (top to bottom): La Mussarra · Mont-ral · Arbolí · Siurana · **Montsant** · Vilanova de Prades · La Riba · Cogullons · Margalef

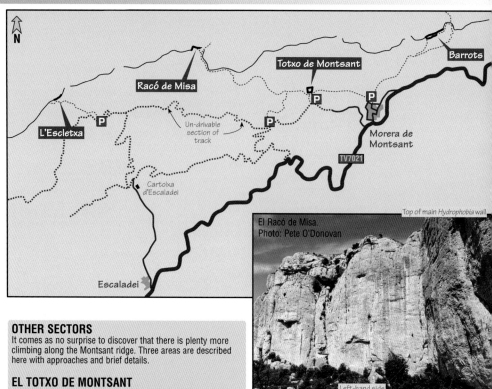

Top of main *Hydrophobia* wall

El Racó de Misa.
Photo: Pete O'Donovan

Left-hand side with 4 routes

Left-hand side of main wall

OTHER SECTORS

It comes as no surprise to discover that there is plenty more climbing along the Montsant ridge. Three areas are described here with approaches and brief details.

EL TOTXO DE MONTSANT

A free standing boulder with a handful or routes. *Photo page 11.*
APPROACH (See map) - From La Morera de Montsant take TV-7021 towards Escaladei (Scala Dei). After 100m turn right onto narrow track (surfaced at first). After about 1km a there is a small parking place on the right from which a path leads up to the obvious giant boulder - El Totxo. 10-15 min walk.

EL RACO DE MISA

This amazing crag has become internationally famous over the past few years because of the route *Hydrophobia*. The photo to the right shows one of the superb walls of this crag.
APPROACH - Approach as for El Totxo but continue along the track for another 1km (approx) until you see an obvious path on the right with a red and white marker painted on a rock. Follow the path until it splits then take the left-hand fork to El Raco. (20-30 mins walk).
Note: you will know if you have missed the parking spot for El Raco de Misa because shortly afterwards the track deteriorates and begins to descend very steeply - don't go there!

THE ROUTES

Only a few details are known and development is continuing so these details might be out-of-date.
Left-hand wall (*photo opposite of the 6c*) - Four long vertical pitches. L to R - 7a+, 7a, 6c+, 6c.
Main wall - The left-hand side of this wall is steep but not as steep as the awesome right-hand section. L to R - ?, 7b+, 7b+, 7c, ?. Then things get really steep. Also these pitches are 40m to 50m long - ? with 8a RH branch, 8a, 8a+ (*Carnaleta*), 7c+, 8b+ (*Hydrophobia*), ?, 7c.

L'ESCLETXA

Another impressive crag with a small set of quality routes.
APPROACH - From La Morera de Montsant take the TV-7021 to Escladei (Scala Dei) and from here take a small road signposted Cartoixa d'Escaladei (a ruined monastery which is undergoing renovations). Continue along this road, which is now unsurfaced, taking a left at the first junction and a right at the second. This is all part of the GR 171. This takes you to a parking space with a metal sign that says 'Castell de Rius' and 'El Grau de L'Escletxa'. (About 2.5k from La Cartoixa). Follow the path up towards the rocks then walk rightwards until an overhanging wall guarded by a large roof is reached. This is it! (20min walk).

THE ROUTES

The 6 routes on the main section have undercut starts. L to R - 7c+, 7c+, 7c+, 8a+, 8b, 8a. There are 2 6b's further right.

ROCA CORBATERA

From El Falco and the top of Siurana, one feature stands out above all others on the Montsant ridge. This is the open-book corner of Roca Corbatera. This has been developed with a few routes although there is much more still to be done. No further details are known except that the routes are bound to be good.
APPROACH - From Cornudella take the C242 to Albarca (see general map on page 30). Leave the car just beyond the village and follow the wide path (GR 171) along the Serra de Montsant ridge for 2km. Where the main path heads off rightwards continue along the crest for a further 500m to the cliff. (About 45mins walk).

ndy Cave on the right-hand 6c of the left-
nd wall at El Racó de Misa at Montsant.
posite. Photo: Pete O'Donovan

VILANOVA DE PRADES

La Mussarra

Mont-ral

Arbolí

Siurana

Montsant

Vilanova de Prades

La Riba

Cogullons

Margalef

The first impression of the crags surrounding the village of Vilanova de Prades may be one of déja vu for British climbers since their appearance from a distance is similar to the Peak District's gritstone edges. However this is the only similarity as, apart from their dimensions, the climbing style is totally different. The rock is a conglomerate that has been coated with a limestone tufa, a combination that provides an exceptional climbing medium. The holds are almost exclusively good pockets of all sizes and the gear is fine and sensibly spaced. Nevertheless the style of the climbing takes some getting used to so, to avoid any tendon or forearm blowouts, start slowly and don't head straight onto the harder grades. The setting for the crags is typical of this area with olive and walnut groves littering the terraced hillsides. Another attraction is the proximity of a full-facilities campground complete with restaurant, bar and pool, directly below the Camping Crags. This site would be a great base for families or teams who like a camping holiday atmos-

Emma Medara on *Equinox* (6b) on Sector Camping at Vilanova de Prades. *Page 135.* Photo: Highroglyphics

phere but would prefer to be away from the coast and like a bit of luxury not always found at the refuges. The owners of the campsite are themselves climbers and sell some kit as well as having a new routes topo in their bar.

THE ROUTES

The Vilanova crags offer routes to cater for most holidaying sport climbers, from slabby grade 4s through to severely overhanging pocket-pulling 8s. The climbs are between 15 and 20m long and are extremely sustained, offering little in the way of decent ledges or breaks in the angle of the rock. Strong lines are also in evidence with some of the best mid-grade climbs following corners and cracks. If you are on a limited time budget the best spot to head for is Sector Camping which has enough great pitches to keep anyone happy for a day or two. For those who like steep rock Sector Del Ploms will not disappoint. The most diverse sector in terms of grades and rock angle is that of Llena with some classic easy slabs and mega 7c+ and 8a pumpouts. Most of the rock is solid but the odd sections have less-well-cemented pebbles should be treated with care.

⊖ Some of the bolts have been removed from the Out of Town crags by an irate landowner. People do still climb there but it is best to check at the camp site first.

CONDITIONS

All the crags face due south, although certain sections will get a little shade at the beginning or end of the day. Generally though this is a warm venue. It is at an altitude of 1000m but is a good spot to head for if the areas nearer the coast are covered in mist. Climbing in the rain is possible at Dels Ploms and La Llena.

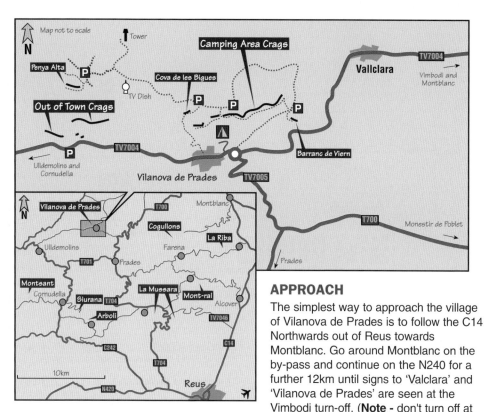

APPROACH

The simplest way to approach the village of Vilanova de Prades is to follow the C14 Northwards out of Reus towards Montblanc. Go around Montblanc on the by-pass and continue on the N240 for a further 12km until signs to 'Valclara' and 'Vilanova de Prades' are seen at the Vimbodi turn-off. (**Note -** don't turn off at the first sign to Vimbodi but stay on the main road for another 1km or so - this avoids Vimbodi centre.) Follow the road (T-7004) through Valclara and up to Vilanova de Prades in 10km. Vilanova de Prades can also be reached from Siurana on the C242 to Ulldemolins. From La Mussara, Vilanova de Prades is around 30 minutes by car on the T-704 through the villages of Febro and Prades (not to be confused with Vilanova de Prades).

LOCAL FACILITIES

Vilanova de Prades has a number of small shops, and a restaurant/bar by the roundabout. The Campsite also has a small shop and a bar and restaurant, and some nice cabins which would be an attractive option in the middle of winter.

Check in the bar at campsite for latest news on route development. Also it is possible to walk from the campsite to the Camping Sectors but check in the bar topos regarding access as the paths cross private land.

LOCAL TOPO GUIDE

There is a small guidebook available from the campsite at Vilanova de Prades which covers all the routes here plus Sectors Penya Alta, Cova de Bigues and Barranc de Viern which are marked on the map above and on the next page. This may well be updated soon to cover the new routes to the right of Sector Camping.

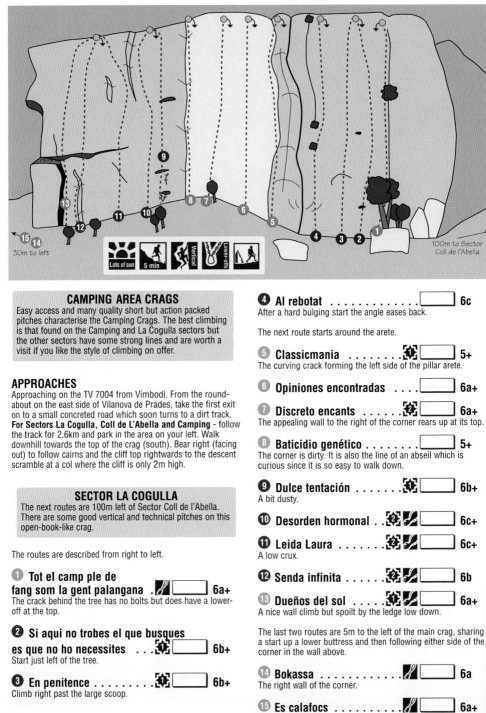

30m to left

Lots of sun | 5 min | Vertical | Lower-offs

100m to Sector
Coll de l'Abella

La Mussarra · Mont-ral · Arbolí · Siurana · Montsant · Vilanova de Prades · La Riba · Cogullons · Margalef

CAMPING AREA CRAGS
Easy access and many quality short but action packed pitches characterise the Camping Crags. The best climbing is that found on the Camping and La Cogulla sectors but the other sectors have some strong lines and are worth a visit if you like the style of climbing on offer.

APPROACHES
Approaching on the TV 7004 from Vimbodi. From the round-about on the east side of Vilanova de Prades, take the first exit on to a small concreted road which soon turns to a dirt track. **For Sectors La Cogulla, Coll de L'Abella and Camping** - follow the track for 2.6km and park in the area on your left. Walk downhill towards the top of the crag (south). Bear right (facing out) to follow cairns and the cliff top rightwards to the descent scramble at a col where the cliff is only 2m high.

SECTOR LA COGULLA
The next routes are 100m left of Sector Coll de l'Abella. There are some good vertical and technical pitches on this open-book-like crag.

The routes are described from right to left.

**① Tot el camp ple de
fang som la gent palangana** . . . 6a+
The crack behind the tree has no bolts but does have a lower-off at the top.

**② Si aqui no trobes el que busques
es que no ho necessites** . . . 6b+
Start just left of the tree.

③ En penitence . . . . 6b+
Climb right past the large scoop.

④ Al rebotat 6c
After a hard bulging start the angle eases back.

The next route starts around the arete.

⑤ Classicmania . . . . 5+
The curving crack forming the left side of the pillar arete.

⑥ Opiniones encontradas . . . . 6a+

⑦ Discreto encants . . . . . . 6a+
The appealing wall to the right of the corner rears up at its top.

⑧ Baticidio genético . . . . 5+
The corner is dirty. It is also the line of an abseil which is curious since it is so easy to walk down.

⑨ Dulce tentación . . . . . . 6b+
A bit dusty.

⑩ Desorden hormonal . . 6c+

⑪ Leida Laura . . . . 6c+
A low crux.

⑫ Senda infinita 6b

⑬ Dueños del sol . . . . . 6a+
A nice wall climb but spoilt by the ledge low down.

The last two routes are 5m to the left of the main crag, sharing a start up a lower buttress and then following either side of the corner in the wall above.

⑭ Bokassa 6a
The right wall of the corner.

⑮ Es calafocs . . . . 6a+
The left wall of the corner.

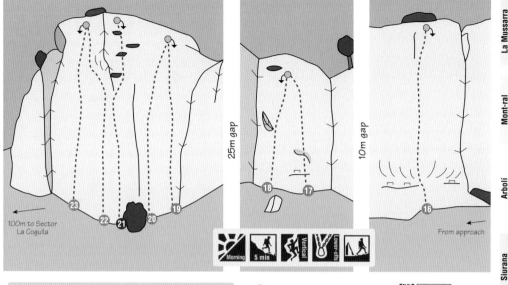

100m to Sector
La Cogulla

25m gap

10m gap

From approach

La Mussarra
Mont-ral
Arbolí
Siurana
Montsant
Vilanova de Prades
La Riba
Cogullons
Margalef

SECTOR COLL DE L'ABELLA

The first routes you arrive at as you walk rightwards (facing out) along the crag are on the uninpressive Sector Coll de l'Abella.

The routes are described from right to left.

16 Eslapillo final . . . . ☐ 6a+

17 Barrancos . . . . 🗝☐ 6a+
A poor and uninspiring piece of rock.

18 Trancos . . . . 🗝☐ 5
More poor rock, walk on by.

19 Xiclets de Reus . . . . ☐ 5

20 Saltin camping . . . . ☐ 5

21 A vista despista . . . 🔲🔲☐ 6b+

22 A.D.F . . . . 🔲🔲☐ 6a+
The best of the trio.

23 Drassana . . . . 🔲🔲☐ 5

PENYA ALTA
An excellent sector on the top of the hill. Drive past the TV mast and park at the top. Walk south (downhil) towards the crag. (See map on page 131). There are 29 routes with plenty of easy stuff (grade 4 and 5) on the far left-hand side of the main section. The rest are between 6a+ and 7b+. See local topo for more.

COVA DE LES BIGUES
Situated above and left of Sector La Cogulla, a crag of two contrasting halfs. 11 routes on the left-hand side which gradually increase in grade from 4+ to 6b. Then a steep cave with 8 hard routes from 7b+ to 8b+. See local topo for more.

BARRANC DE VIERN
Situated below the approach track from the parking for Sector Pitufos. A good crag with plenty of easy routes. 15 routes from 4+ to 6b+. from the left-hand end, routes 3 to 8 are all in the 4+/5+ range. See local topo for more.

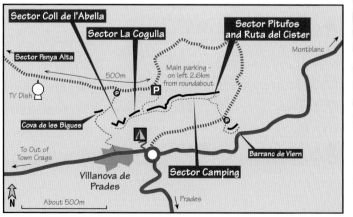

Sector Coll de l'Abella
Sector La Cogulla
Sector Pitufos and Ruta del Cister
Montblanc
Sector Penya Alta
Main parking - on left 2.6km from roundabout
500m
TV Dish
Cova de les Bigues
Barranc de Viern
To Out of Town Crags
Villanova de Prades
Sector Camping
Prades
About 500m
N

133

La Mussara

Mont-ral

Arbolí

Siurana

Montsant

Vilanova de Prades

La Riba

Cogullons

Margalef

SECTOR CAMPING - Left

There is a good variety of routes on the left-hand sector ranging from some amenable 5s to steep grooves with the odd hand jam and a cluster of more power packed 7s.

APPROACH FROM BELOW - It is possible to walk from the campsite to the Camping Sectors but check in the bar topos regarding access since the paths cross private land.

1 **Borregos** . . . . **5+**

2 **Pastelada** **6a**

3 **La Cachadeta** **7b**

4 **Cabrita** **6a**

5 **Carbronada** **6b**

6 **Cabra** . . . . **6a+**
A tasty piece of jamming up the steep crackline.

7 **Esto es un infierno** . . **7b+**

8 **Damian** **6c**
Ever fancied *Profit of Doom* with bolts? This looks like it is a touch bolder!

9 **Nasadaravia** **7a**
Fine technical wall climbing.

10 **La vista del tio santi** . . . . **6b+**

11 **Kira** . . . . **6c+**

12 **O'Tiny** **7b**

13 **Patiada al cul** . . . . . . **7b+**
Start up the tufa stain.

14 **Gina** **7c**

15 **Caligula** **7c**
The thin discontinuous crack to start.

16 **Bad Boy Junior** . . **7c**

17 **Dano** **7b**

18 **Dragon kan** **7a**
An attractive pitch taking a diagonal line up the impressive bulging wall.

19 **La novatada** **6c**

20 **Vampinglandià** **6a**

21 **Els impresentables** . . **7a+**

22 **Tot fang** **6c**

SECTOR CAMPING - Middle

You can work your way along this great selection of grade 6s ticking as many as your tendons will allow. The excellent bridging corner of *Supersonix* will bring a much needed rest from the pocket pulling.

23 Pitufo ros . . . . **5+**
The shallow corner just right of the arete.

24 Makamanu **6c**

25 Kriminal de muntanya **6c**
A fantastic wall climb which shouldn't be missed.

26 White Shark . . . . **6a+**

27 Complete supramolecular . . **6b**

28 J.M. Jarre **6b**
Eases off after the first half.

29 Mossen . . . . . . **6a+**
Sustained climbing via the large pocket.

30 Supersonix . . . . **6a+**
The fine right-angle corner. Sustained bridging leads to a final pull left to the lower-off.

31 Conciencia transparente . **6c**
Gets tough just below the top.

32 Fina i segura . . . . . **7a+**

33 Revolution . . . . **6a+**

34 Equinoxe **6b**
Photo on page 130 and 137.

35 Maneta xafardera . **6b+**
The left-hand side of the dominating rounded arete. Excellent and very photogenic.

SECTOR CAMPING - Right

The bulging grey wall at the right-hand end should not be missed, especially the absorbing pitch of *Bava de oro*.

36 Ziperman **6c**
Start from the belay bolt just beyond the drop off and climb straight up the scooped arete.

37 Cronologia **7a**
Start as for *Ziper Man*. A superb pitch on good holds and with magnificent views. A must!

38 Baya de oro **7b**
Start from the lowest point of the buttress and take the unbroken line of pockets up the otherwise blank wall. A stunning pitch.

39 Tom Bombadil . . . . . **7a+**

40 Fingolfin **6c**
After a steep start finish up the smart curving groove.

41 Tattoo . . . . **7b+**

42 Buff!! **8a**

43 Al lorut . . . . **7c+**
The right-hand side of the arete.

44 Aventura placal . . . . **6c+**
Short crack and wall.

45 Barri jeu . . . . **5+**

46 Biceps letargados . . . . **6a+**
The crack line.

47 Inef-tes **7a**
Start up *Biceps* and break right onto the wall.

To the right are some very new routes - check at the camp site.

La Mussara
Mont-ral
Arbolí
Siurana
Montsant
Vilanova de Prades
La Riba
Cogullons
Margalef

La Mussara

Mont-ral

Arbolí

Siurana

Montsant

Vilanova de Prades

La Riba

Cogullons

Margalef

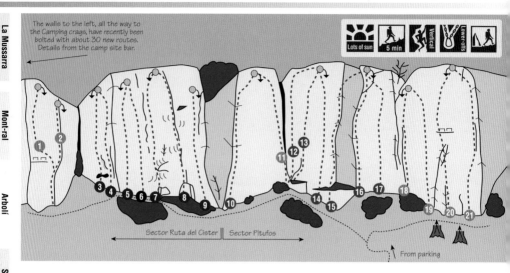

The walls to the left, all the way to the Camping crags, have recently been bolted with about 30 new routes. Details from the camp site bar.

Lots of sun | 5 min | Vertical | Lower-offs

Sector Ruta del Cister || *Sector Pitufos*

From parking

SECTOR RUTA DEL CISTER
The penultimate sectors along this escarpment of crags offer contrasting climbing styles. The classic route is the one with the strongest line - *Parawoll-Damm*.

APPROACH - see map on page 133
From the roundabout in Vilanova de Prades, follow the dirt track for 1km. Park on the right at a small pull-off. Cross over the track and follow the rock bedding and then take a path on the right uphill towards to the crags.

1 Saburella **6a**
After stepping off the ledge, this short route is almost over.

2 Trenca olles . . . . **5+**
The gaping crack is only short lived - thankfully?

3 Flipe Gonzalez . . . . . **6c+**
All the pockets seemed to have disappeared on this wall

4 La ruta del cister . . . **7a**
The headwall rears up at you as you tussle with the thin crack.

5 Ton Sawyer . . . . **6b+**
After a butch start the climbing above is very enjoyable.

6 La batalla del verano . . . **7a+**

7 Ares **6c**

8 Parawoll-damm **6c**
Good territory for the trad climber to get to grips with digging up those crack techniques - show those sport climbers a thing or two!

9 A pio pio pam pam . . **6c+**
Is this an affectionate name for someone's loved one? A very photogenic arete with some brilliant pocket pulling.

SECTOR PITUFOS
The wall right of the corner has high first bolts.

10 Poblet . . . . **4+**
Quite tricky especially low down before you can bridge out.

11 Roc penat **5**
Excellent route around bulges - need to think.

12 Solana . . . . **4+**
Bridging helps as it's quite steep in places.

13 Magali . . . . **4+**
Technical finish but a good climb.

14 Aniuski . . . . **4+**
Tricky start.

15 Tonin **4**
1st bolt removed. Makes for a tricky and bold start, great climbing above with a nice finish.

16 Too . . . . **4+**
Fantastic route, better than *Poblet*. Spaced bolts.

17 Pitufos . . . . **4+**
A good route with spaced bolts. Go left at the 2nd bolt or you will encounter some very tricky moves.

18 Maite **5**
Not such good rock.

19 Makoski **5**
Very hard finish (left) at the top.

20 Emboscada . . . . **5+**

21 Arpo . . . . **5+**
Nice climbing.

La Mussara

Mont-ral

Arboli

Siurana

Montsant

Vilanova de Prades

La Riba

Cogullons

Margalef

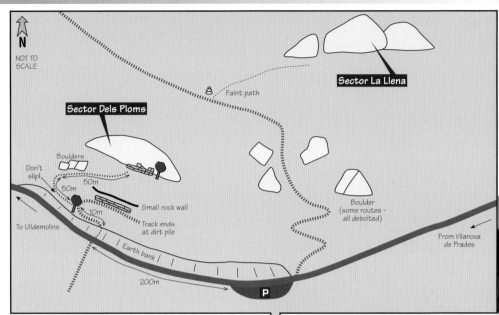

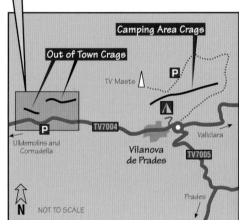

OUT OF TOWN CRAGS
The Out of Town Crags are beautifully located to the west of Vilanova de Prades and have a good number of routes for those climbing 4s and 5s. There is then a dearth of middle grade routes before kicking in again at the higher grades.

APPROACH TO SECTOR LA LLENA
From Vilanova de Prades drive towards Ulldemolins for 3.5km, which is between the 7km and 6km markers. Park in a pull-off on the left. The crag is visible directly up the hill from the pull-out. From the Vilanova de Prades end of the pullout, cross over the road and scramble up the mud slope. Follow a cairned path as it zig-zags towards some big Totxos (boulders). The first one on your right, Totxo Peñita, has five routes. The path weaves through the boulders and then continues in a westerly direction. Look out for a faint path marked with a cairn which forks right from the main trail and leads up to the crag after about 100m.

APPROACH TO SECTOR DELS PLOMS
From the La Llena parking pull-out, walk down the road towards Ulldemolins, for 200m. The crag is very obvious at this point from the road. On the opposite side of the road to a dirt track scramble up the earth bank. Turn immediately left and walk along an old road for 10m. Just as the road bends r as the road bends rrrrd bends round to the right a faint path leads off left past a tree. Follow this as it heads uphill through scratchy vegetation. After 50m, at some boulders, the path bends right. Continue for another 50m until you are at the crag.

🚫 ACCESS
Since the publication of the last guidebook the local landowner has decided that he no longer wishes people to climb at the Out of Town Crags. He has smashed the low bolts of some routes and removed the lower-offs he can reach. The routes are included in this book just in case the situation improves. For more information you should talk to the owners of the campsite at Vilanova de Prades.

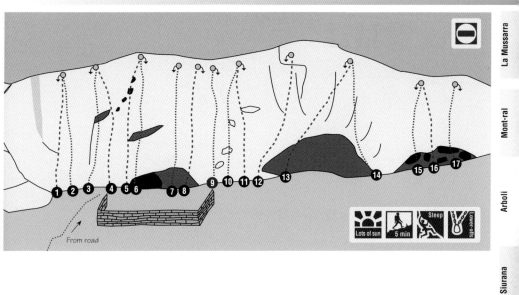

From road

Lots of sun | 5 min | Steep | Lower-offs

La Mussarra

Mont-ral

Arboli

Siurana

Montsant

Vilanova de Prades

La Riba

Cogullons

Margalef

SECTOR DELS PLOMS

An attractive bulging buttress, streaked with limestone deposits and home to no easy routes.

⊖ Some of the low bolts on these routes have been smashed and a few of the lower-offs are missing. Some of the low bolts are still clippable and you can find alternative belays. A large Friend or two might be found useful for the large pockets to protect the lower sections of the routes.

❶ Alua 7b
Spoilt by a ledge.

❷ Miss-to 8a
An immaculate wall which is well worth seeking out.

❸ Yin-yang .... 7b+
Another appealing line. *Photo on page 8.*

❹ Fukuoka ..... 8b+

❺ Electric buda 8b

❻ Spider 8b

❼ Indian Tattoo 8b
Known as Ponte a Brincar in the last book. An inspiring piece of bulging rock which is peppered with small pockets.

❽ The Power of Resin .... 8a+

❾ A la guly he 7a

❿ Follim-follam ... 7a+

⓫ Ali up 7c

⓬ Peligrosa Maria 7c
Start close to the tufa stain. A hard last move.

⓭ Akiko .... 7c+

⓮ Blodhongang 8a

⓯ Pillacin .... 7a+

⓰ Sacrificio .... 7b+

⓱ Splash 7b

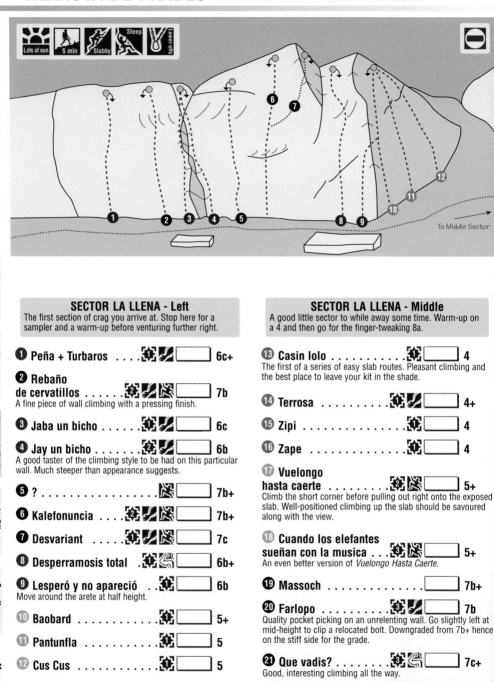

SECTOR LA LLENA - Left

The first section of crag you arrive at. Stop here for a sampler and a warm-up before venturing further right.

① Peña + Turbaros . . . . 🔲🔲 6c+

② Rebaño de cervatillos . . . . . 🔲🔲🔲 7b
A fine piece of wall climbing with a pressing finish.

③ Jaba un bicho . . . . . . 🔲🔲 6c

④ Jay un bicho . . . . . . 🔲🔲 6b
A good taster of the climbing style to be had on this particular wall. Much steeper than appearance suggests.

⑤ ? . . . . 🔲 7b+

⑥ Kalefonuncia . . . . 🔲🔲🔲 7b+

⑦ Desvariant . . . . . 🔲🔲🔲 7c

⑧ Desperramosis total . 🔲🔲 6b+

⑨ Lesperó y no apareció . . 🔲 6b
Move around the arete at half height.

⑩ Baobard . . . . 🔲 5+

⑪ Pantunfla . . . . 🔲 5

⑫ Cus Cus . . . . 🔲 5

SECTOR LA LLENA - Middle

A good little sector to while away some time. Warm-up on a 4 and then go for the finger-tweaking 8a.

⑬ Casin lolo . . . . 🔲 4
The first of a series of easy slab routes. Pleasant climbing and the best place to leave your kit in the shade.

⑭ Terrosa . . . . 🔲🔲 4+

⑮ Zipi . . . . 🔲 4

⑯ Zape . . . . 🔲 4

⑰ Vuelongo hasta caerte . . . . 🔲🔲 5+
Climb the short corner before pulling out right onto the exposed slab. Well-positioned climbing up the slab should be savoured along with the view.

⑱ Cuando los elefantes sueñan con la musica . . . 🔲🔲 5+
An even better version of *Vuelongo Hasta Caerte*.

⑲ Massoch . . . . 🔲 7b+

⑳ Farlopo . . . . 🔲🔲 7b
Quality pocket picking on an unrelenting wall. Go slightly left at mid-height to clip a relocated bolt. Downgraded from 7b+ hence on the stiff side for the grade.

㉑ Que vadis? . . . . 🔲🔲 7c+
Good, interesting climbing all the way.

㉒ Orgasmotron . . . . . . 🔲🔲 8a
Fancy the ride? Make sure you're good and ready for the hard start.

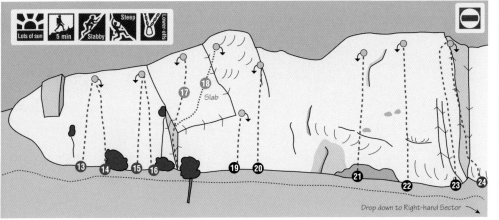

Drop down to Right-hand Sector

23 Fanatic cloc . . . . 🎿🎿 ⬜ **7a+**
An unbalanced route with a bouldery start and less sustained climbing above.

24 Pensaments ocults . . 🎿🎿 ⬜ **6c+**
Similar to *Fanatic Cloc* with a seemingly impossible move off the deck.

SECTOR LA LLENA - Right
The next routes appear 30m to the right on a huge, bulging, impressive hunk of rock. If you are wanting a workout, head for this end.

25 L'ultim gong . . . . 🎿🎿🎿 ⬜ **7c+**
Sustained climbing up the very steep tufa crack. Just keep moving.

26 Pulsar . . . . 🎿🎿🎿 ⬜ **8a+**
Very steep again heading for the cluster of holes above.

27 Tuncatumpà . . . . ⬜ **8b**

28 ? . . . . ⬜ **8b+**

29 Megapubilla . . . . 🎿🎿🎿 ⬜ **8a**
Climbing through the series of small wiggly cracks and continuing above to the right of the dead tree.

30 Project . . . . ⬜
A long term project.

The next two routes are 5m to the right on the lesser bulging buttress climbing either side of a thin crack.

31 Esperense que ahora . . . . ⬜ **7c+**

32 Alhambra . . . . ⬜ **7c+**

🚫 ACCESS
The land owner doesn't want people to climb on this crag. On all three buttresses some of the low bolts have been smashed and a few of the lower-offs are missing. Some of the low bolts are still clippable and you can find alternative belays. A large Friend or two might be found useful for the large pockets to protect the lower sections of the routes.

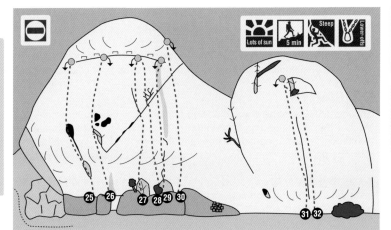

La Mussarra

Mont-ral

Arboli

Siurana

Montsant

Vilanova de Prades

La Riba

Cogullons

Margalef

LA RIBA

La Mussarra

Mont-ral

Arbolí

Siurana

Montsant

Vilanova de Prades

La Riba

Cogulons

Margalef

Penya Roja

Sector
La Directa

Sector
Les Plaques

Sector
Sense Nom

Sector Xina

Sector
Pedestal

The main sectors at La Riba. Photo: Highroglyphics

The impressive boulder-choked valley that restrains the river Brugent for much of its length between the town of La Riba and the perfectly proportioned hamlet of La Farena, is lined with limestone cliffs. The winding single track road that hugs the river's edge gives easy access to many of the crags which have been developed along the valley, but supreme amongst these is the formation of Penya Roja. The Penya Roja contains the earliest routes of the region being easily accessed and offering what must have been an irresistible challenge to earlier pioneers. Today the four main sectors on the Penya, and its flanking sister crag of Xina, give the present day sport climber a choice of over a hundred routes of up to 4 pitches. There is something for every climber here except for those operating in the highest grades. Indeed for those wanting 5s, 6s and 7s you could do worse than spend a week's holiday here alone. Many visiting climbers from outside Spain have been reluctant to try La Riba since it was wrongly credited by a French selected guide as being located in an industrial setting. The town of La Riba itself is home to some industrial complexes but is a good distance from the actual crags.

THE ROUTES

Soaring pillars, leaning walls, slabs and bulging pocketed buttresses - La Riba has them all. Much of the climbing is on blank pocketed walls interspersed by small stances, however many of the routes' first and second pitches offer the best climbing and can be climbed and lowered off in one long pitch on a 60m rope. The longest routes are on the La Directa, Sense Nom and Les Plaque sectors.

Sector Pedestal is small but has a trio of fine 6s which should not be missed. Sector Xina was once the venue for a climbing competition and has a number of brilliant 'designer' routes on which you can test your skills against the grades of yesteryear.

CONDITIONS
The main climbing on all of the sectors faces south-east and is therefore shaded from mid afternoon onwards but generally the area has a sunny feel about it. It can get very warm on the open faces although the base of the crag offers ample shade to cool off aprés route. The crags of La Riba are the lowest lying in the guide and are therefore a good bet in cold or poor weather. The crags dry almost instantly after rain but do not offer much in the way of totally sheltered climbing if it is actually raining. If it does really start to throw it down go careful crossing the normally dry riverbed, those bus-sized boulders only got to where they are by the power of water. After several days of rain the river can become impassable.

LOCAL FACILITIES
There is a free official camping area, equipped with tables, just down the hill from the parking area . Most of the time the site is quiet but it can become extremely overcrowded and depressingly filthy on, and after, public holidays. Potable water can be obtained from two fonts located just down the road from the parking. The first is in the camping area. Limited wild camping can be had on the approach to the crag in cleared areas but even here you may not get a lot of rest on weekends and public holidays. There is little of much interest in La Riba except for a bakery near the church. It is better to shop, eat and drink in Montblanc. There is also a nice restaurant at Farena.

APPROACH
The town of La Riba is easily reached from Reus or Montblanc on the C14. Take the La Riba and Farena exit and follow the winding road up through the town until the road levels out and the formation of the main crag can be seen ahead. Continue along the road for a further 1.5km to an obvious parking area on the left below a large man-made wall. Opposite the parking area, and on the far side of the river bed, is an attractive derelict building shaded by palm trees. The path to all sectors drops down from the road into the riverbed and ascends towards the crags to the left of this derelict building (facing the building).
La Riba can also be accessed from the interior of the Sierra de Prades by following the picturesque road from Farena.

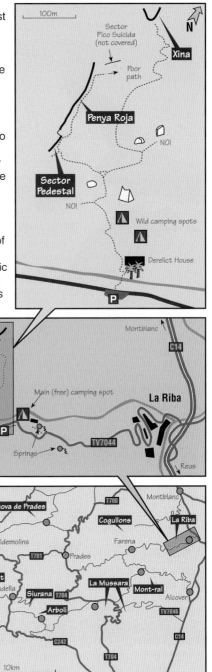

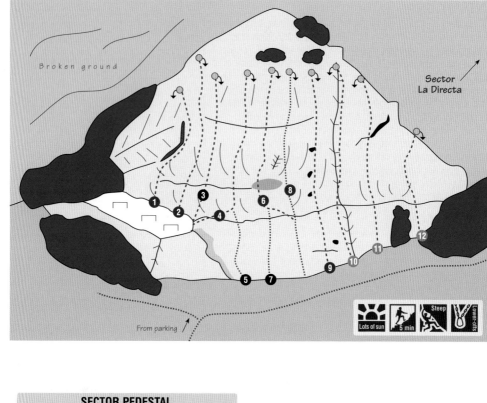

La Mussara

Mont-ral

Arbolí

Siurana

Montsant

Vilanova de Prades

La Riba

Cogullons

Margalef

SECTOR PEDESTAL

You may be itching to launch yourself at the towering buttress of Directa but it is worth stopping en route at the first crag you arrive at. Sector Pedestal has a number of excellent climbs, particularly *Menjar menjant*, *La via de Bryan* and *Eclipse*. The polish is testament to the popularity of these routes.

❶ Hakuna matata 6c
Brutal.

❷ Curt i distant 7a
Short and sharp.

❸ Mala baba . . . . 7b+

❹ La chica de la puerta 16 . . . . 7a
Keep going at the same pace you start at and you may just reach the anchors.

❺ Direct start . . . . 7b+
Polished and hard.

❻ Más difficil todavia . . . 7a
The main challenge of the bulging buttress.

❼ Direct start . . . . 7b+
Another desperate and polished direct start.

❽ Menjar menjant . . 6c
A tricky and slick start gives access to brilliant pocket pulling on the upper wall. Tricky for the grade.

❾ La via de Bryan . . 6b+
A superb jug-fest with a slippery start. Excellent at the top.

❿ Eclipse . . . . 6a+
Tasty climbing whetting your appetite for more.

⓫ Circulo vicioso 6a

⓬ Ho sento molt 5

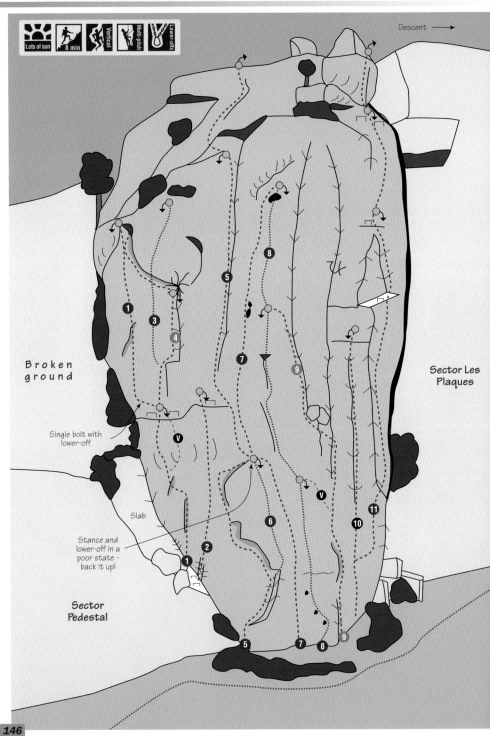

Lots of sun • 8 min • Vertical • Multi-pitch • Lower-offs

Descent →

La Mussara

Mont-ral

Arbolí

Siurana

Montsant

Vilanova de Prades

La Riba

Cogullons

Margalef

Broken
ground

Single bolt with
lower-off

Slab

Stance and
lower-off in a
poor state -
back it up!

Sector
Pedestal

Sector Les
Plaques

PENYA ROJA - SECTOR LA DIRECTA

The impressive orange towering buttress of La Directa dominates the Brugent Valley as you approach the crags of La Riba. This cliff is jam-packed with single and multi-pitch classics and one day alone will not be enough for this cliff as you gradually discover the treasures here. A couple of gems to get you on your way are *Directissima* and *Missio Impossible*.

❶ Karrum 6c

Good climbing with fine views.
1) 6c. An awkward pitch with some difficult and strenuous climbing interspersed with good rests. Belay on the single bolt on the vegetated ledge to the left.
2) 6c. After grappling with the spiky bush, you soon find yourself grappling with the spiky rock. A distinctive blind, fingery crux sequence punctuates the halfway mark of this pitch.

❷ Cal Fer-Ho 7a

A real squeezed-in job but it has plenty of good moves which are a touch reachy in places. Makes a good first pitch to link up with route *Chorben Nuden*.

❸ Chorben Nuden . . 7a

Skidaddle right past the first two bolts and move back left to the third bolt. Then head up the continuously fingery and prickly rock. A great position.

❹ Magi 6a

The start of this route may be reached by scrambling up the leftward-trending, vegetated ramp-line.
1) 6a. The corner crack leads to the belay next to the large dead-looking tree.
2) 6a. The leftward-curving undercut flake leads to an abseil point.

❺ Figuerola-Magriñá 6b

A great route which follows a wild line and is the best way to get the summit experience. Although the route has much fixed gear it is a good idea to take a decent rack to make things safe. Feels more like E3 5c.
1) 6a+. Wild laybacking leads to easier climbing and a cramped stance with poor fixed gear.
2) 6b. Move up leftwards to the obvious broken corner. This is followed all the way to a stance beneath the capping overhang.
3) 5. Move out leftwards and follow the crack back rightwards and up to the summit area.

❻ Directa 6c

A difficult variation first pitch to route *Figuerola-Magriñá*.

❼ Becon Legal . . . . 6b+

A route that seems to have no line of its own, making use of holds on neighbouring routes. The bolts look like relics from the past. Move on.
1) 6b+.
2) 6b+. A vegetated pitch.

❽ Directa Reus . . . . . 6b+

The major line on this section of crag gives very sustained and quite strenuous climbing. Pitch 3 is not often climbed and a little run-out. If you have a 60m rope, running the first two pitches together makes a great route. *Photo on page 5.*
1) 6b+. The pockets are good but good foot friction is lacking.
2) 6b+. The thin cracks above are steep and sustained.
3) 6b+. Difficult moves up the overhanging wall to the left of the stance with some run-out climbing on slightly friable rock.

❾ Directissima . . . . . 6a+

This route is now described as one pitch, the top pitch being overgrown. Follow the shallow corner and good cracks above to a step left at some large flakes/blocks. More steep climbing up the crack system soon leads to a lower-off on the left.

❿ Missió Impossible 7a+

If you are going well, ignore the name. An immaculate pitch on which it is well worth trying for the on-sight.

⓫ Didac . . . . 6b+

1) 6b+. It is best to start up the first 4 bolts of *Missió Impossible*, then step right to join the true line. Some steep and tricky climbing gives way to some run-out moves above a large ledge (and a little moment).
2) 6a. Follow the only bolted line up rightwards to a belay beneath the obvious steep crack.
3) 6b+. The desperate crack to finish. Walk off.

DESCENT FROM SUMMIT - Walk rightwards (facing in) to eventually meet up with a prickly path which leads to Sector Xina. Make sure you wear a good pair of trousers for the walk off.

PENYA ROJA - Squirrels

Recently a small but dedicated bunch of climbers have taken up permanent residence at Penya Roja; a colony of red squirrels. They can climb anywhere on the crag and may surprise you by suddenly appearing out of pockets and then gliding gracefully to the ground. Don't try and out climb them though; you haven't got a chance.

La Mussarra

Mont-ral

Arbolí

Siurana

Montsant

Vilanova de Prades

La Riba

Cogullons

Margalef

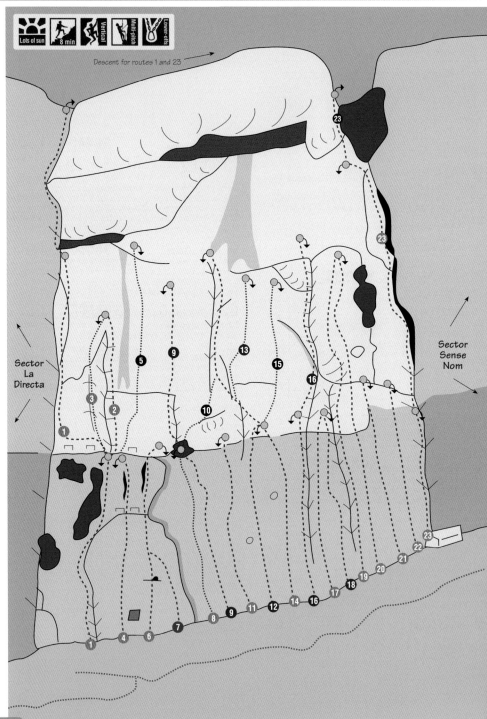

Descent for routes 1 and 23

Sector La Directa

Sector Sense Nom

La Mussarra

Mont-ral

Arbolí

Siurana

Montsant

Vilanova de Prades

La Riba

Cogullons

Margalef

PENYA ROJA - SECTOR LES PLAQUES

Just to the right of Sector La Directa is a wonderful grey angled slab with a plaque on its lower left base. The lower slab provides some excellent moderate lines, either giving quality routes to the midway stances, or to provide access to the upper wall. The upper part of the wall above the slab rears up and provides a number of superb leaning wall and groove lines. Many of these routes are 30m long if the intermediate stances/lower-offs are not used so go carefully when descending/lowering off.

1 Canal (normal) 6a
1) **6a**. The first pitch is a bit of a veg garden.
2) **5**.
3) **4+**.

2 Illusion 6a
This is a variation second pitch to *Canal (normal)*. Climbing *Tomahauck* as your first pitch would make this a starred outing. The route does continue to the top of the crag, but best to finish after pitch 2.

3 Pues de moix . . . . 6a+
The blunt arete to the left of pitch 2 of *Illusion*.

4 Tomahauck 6a
Start to the left of the plaque which you may be tempted to utilise on the tricky start - but don't. It only really eases off near the finish.

5 Bernat pudent . . . . . 7a+
Start to the left of the first bolt and move up and right to pockets. Climb the crunchy wall above with much crab-like motion to the lower-off. Best started up *Tomahauck*.

6 HLM 5
Start to the right of the plaque.

7 Batusi . . . . 4+
Join *HLM* after two bolts.

8 Yak 6a
An unbalanced route with a steep start, easy middle section and an awkward finish.

9 Memphis . . . . 6c+
1) **6a+**. A pleasant and technical first pitch which can be done as a route in its own right.
2) **6c+**. After that mild warm-up prepare yourself for the rigours of the sustained wall climbing of the second pitch.

10 Miss Tinguet 7b

11 Rothmans 6a
Brilliant pocket-pulling on great rock. What more do you want?

12 GEAM . . . . 6c+
Two splendid pitches, both worthy of 3 stars. The two pitches climbed as one make a superbly sustained climb but use the intermediate lower-off with anything less than a 60m rope.
1) **5+**. The first pitch is an excellent exercise in steep 5+ pocket pulling. (You can finish here).
2) **6c+**. The top groove and arete provides sustained and unusual climbing with unobvious moves initially.

13 Nit de bruixes . . . 7a
This pitch breaks right out of pitch 2 of *GEAM* and gives well-positioned climbing, on good pockets, leading to a crimpy crux and a sharp upper wall.

14 Primordials . . . . . . 5+
A really good pitch culminating in the blank-looking upper slab. *Photo on page 145.*

15 Casta de galán . . 7a+
An upper pitch to *Primordials*. Tricky moves away from the stance gain large holds but more fingery climbing lies above before the upper slab.

16 Valls 6c
Tremendous climbing taking the striking corner. Don't forget your jamming technique.
1) **5**.
2) **6c**.

17 Jonny Jetta . . . . 6a+
A worthwhile eliminate.

18 Efebo sonriente 6b

19 Aleix 6a
Start up a shallow groove. Can be split at the half way lower-off.

20 Tirate que está bajito . . . 6a
Nicely sustained climbing taking in a pocketed lower section, and a steeper upper section, in a good position. Although the bolts are spaced they are no cause for heart-flutters. (Intermediate lower-off if needed).

21 La lina 5

22 Los que huyeron del terror . . 5+

23 Banzo-saez 5
1) **5**.
2) **5**.
3) **4+**.

La Mussarra

Mont-ral

Arbolí

Siurana

Montsant

Vilanova de Prades

La Riba

Cogullons

Margalef

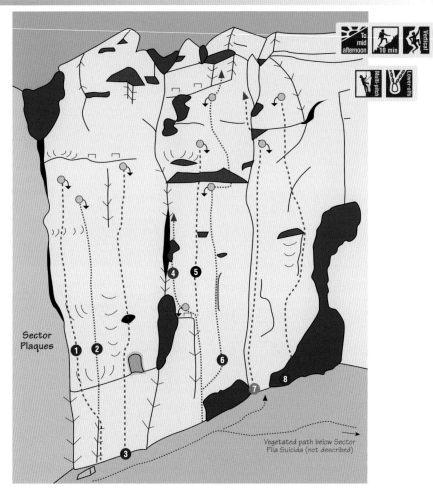

The routes further up the hill to the right on close inspection are of dubious quality and receive little traffic.

PENYA ROJA - SECTOR SENSE NOM
This sector is home to a trio of long fine pitches.

❶ Panini di paura . . . . . 6c+
A route with no distinct crux. A must do!

❷ El mòn màgic del màgic bruffi 7a
After a slightly scrappy start, great climbing up the centre of the pillar. Hard moves low down.

❸ Massagran . . . . . . 6c+
A long pitch with varied climbing on good rock throughout.
Photo opposite

❹ Sense nom . . . . 4+
1) 4+. 2) 4.

❺ Mala pell 7b
Only do if you really have climbed everything else.

❻ De l'Eduard . . . . 6b+
1) 6a+. Poor rock. The anchors below the large overhang are in a poor state.
2) 6b+. Head right from the anchors and over the overhang. Continue up wall above to the left of the large crack.
3) 6b+.

❼ Santacana . . . . 6a+
1) 6a. The big ugly and overgrown crack. 2) 6a+.

❽ Cristo versus Arizona . . . 7a
The start is overgrown but after that is gives a long and interesting pitch.

Massagran (6c+) on Sector Sense Nom, Penya Roja, La Riba. *Opposite.* Photo: Pete O'Donovan

La Mussarra

Mont-ral

Arbolí

Siurana

Montsant

Vilanova de Prades

La Riba

Cogullons

Margalef

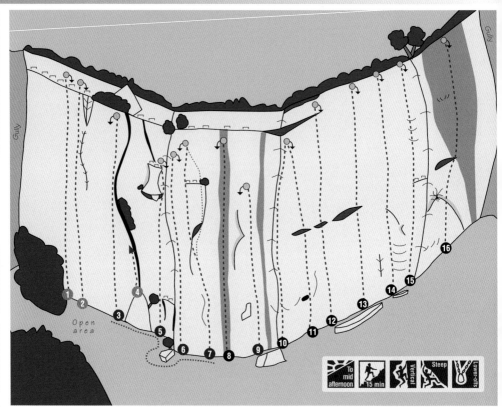

Open area

To mid afternoon | 15 min | Vertical | Steep | Lower-offs

SECTOR XINA

Set further up the hillside from the Penya Roja, and not visible from the car park, Xina keeps its delights well hidden. The best climbing at Xina is in the 7s but there are enough 6s to make the approach worthwhile. Some routes have the odd well-chipped hold but generally these do not spoil the overall experience. It catches any breeze which can make it cooler than elsewhere; ideal for winter mornings in the sun or summer afternoons in the shade.

APPROACH

From the car park follow the path across the river as for the approach to Penya Roja. Once past the derelict house, take the right-hand path. The crag is 10 minutes up the hill, just out of sight.

NOTE: Do not approach Xina from the Penya Roja directly as the path is overgrown and very prickly.

① Marcel . . . . **5+**

② Pilar lagarto **6a**
A good starter.

③ Tian an men . . . . **6b+**

④ Alegre-bonet **5**
The vegetated crack.

⑤ La daga y el puñal . . **6b**
Technical face with good hidden pockets. A good warm-up for the harder routes of this sector.

⑥ Madrid for Ever **6c**
The initial crack should not be missed or under estimated. Cunning use of technique will see you to the top. A good line in a good position. *Photo opposite.*

⑦ Coll torçat **7a**
Not really that pleasant but a good line. A 6c+ variation heads straight up where the 7a branches out right and then up. Same anchors.

Lewis Grundy on *Madrid for Ever* (6c) on Sector Xina at La Riba. *Opposite.* Photo: Alan James

La Mussarra

Mont-ral

Arboli

Siurana

Montsant

Vilanova de Prades

La Riba

Cogullons

Margalef

8 ? . . . . ☐ ?
A line of cemented bolts up the grey streak. Looks good.

9 Codigo de marras . . . . ☐ 6c+

10 Comando violeta . . . .  ☐ 7a+
The arete has some intricate flowstone climbing in its lower section followed by a sequency crux in the overhanging upper arete.

11 Jocs de llit . . . . . 🔲🔲🔲 ☐ 7c
The wall to the right of the arete gives some very thin climbing. A good rest half way up prepares you for the stretchy crux sequence.

12 Vendetta . . . . 🔲🔲 ☐ 7c
The middle of the overhanging east wall has a series of manufactured holds created for a competition many years ago. This artificial relic is still a worthwhile route.

13 Durruti column . . 🔲🔲🔲 ☐ 7c+
Another good pitch with the crux right at the top.

14 Amaneca que
no es poco . . . . 🔲🔲🔲 ☐ 7a+
The steep lower orange rock gives way to less steep but technical climbing on grey rock above with a pumpy last move. A really good outing.

15 Todo es possible
en Domingo . . . . 🔲🔲🔲 ☐ 7b
A disjointed lower section with a hard move one third of the way up. The upper grey wall provides much more continuous climbing.

16 Pecatta minutta . . . . 🔲🔲 ☐ 7c
It is possible to miss out the bouldery start by walkign around to the right.

COGULLONS

La Mussarra

Mont-ral

Arboli

Siurana

Montsant

Vilanova de Prades

La Riba

Cogullons

Margalef

Mark Glasiter and Emma Medara on *Matute* (7a) Mola Roquerola. *Page 161.* Photo: Highroglyphics

Located at 1000m, and approached by a long and rough drive up from the valley town of Montblanc, Cogullons is the most remote and least frequented area covered in this book. However, situation, remoteness and stunning views combine to give the Cogullons area an atmosphere which will appeal to those looking for something a little different away from the more accessible and well-trodden crags of Siurana, La Mussara and La Riba. The approach is not to be taken lightly (or at speed). The drive up and complex crag approaches will eat into a day's climbing time and it may be preferable to plan to spend a couple of days in the Cogullons area if you are flexible. This is complicated by the general lack of facilities (the old refuge has been abandoned) however at least the camping is free.

ACCESS
There is a seasonal ban on climbing because of nesting Eagles.
No climbing between the 1st of January and 1st July.

THE ROUTES
Long undercut waves of creamy-white pocketed rock are to be found at Mola Roquerola with the remains of old dwellings dotting the base. Watch your tendons. In contrast the labyrinth of Les Gralles hides the selection of pocketed walls and aretes. Les Gralles has a good selection of 5s and easier 6s whilst Mola Roquerola caters for those operating in the high 6s and 7s.

CONDITIONS
The Cogullons crags are all located at around 1000m and are therefore cooler than those of Siurana and La Riba. However Mola Roquerola faces south and little shade can be found at the base, as the raised ledge system at the crag base is above the trees. The Les Gralles sectors face south and west and shade can usually be found in amongst the pinnacles.
    Neither of the two venues are good places to be in bad weather.

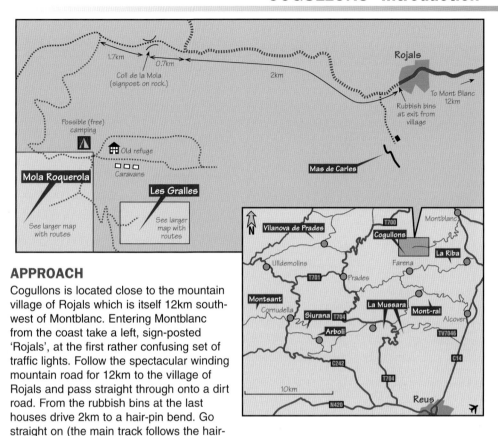

APPROACH

Cogullons is located close to the mountain village of Rojals which is itself 12km south-west of Montblanc. Entering Montblanc from the coast take a left, sign-posted 'Rojals', at the first rather confusing set of traffic lights. Follow the spectacular winding mountain road for 12km to the village of Rojals and pass straight through onto a dirt road. From the rubbish bins at the last houses drive 2km to a hair-pin bend. Go straight on (the main track follows the hair-pin to the right) for 0.7km to the 'Coll de la Mola' marked by a large lump of rounded rock on the right with sign post on top. From the col, continue straight ahead for 1.7km to an unmarked junction and turn sharp left here. Keep going for 1.1km to the parking. The final 500m looks a bit daunting but is okay to drive. The parking is obvious at the base of the approach path up to the unusual looking refuge. The old refuge is perched on a prominent hilltop and can be seen on the left at times from the dirt road after Rojals.

LOCAL FACILITIES

Local facilities are a bit sparse so bring all your food up with you. There are no shops in Rojals and only a very small cafe bar. Some pleasant camping spots can be found close to the parking area at the old refuge. The refuge itself has been abandoned. Water can be found at the font on the approach to Mola Roquerola.

OTHER CRAGS IN THE AREA

There are a number of other crags worth considering.

Mas de Carles - A small crag shown on the map above. It has the advantage of not requiring the tortuous dirt track approach of the other areas. However there are only 14 short routes from grades 6b+ to 7c+

Mola Pastoral - A small crag passed on the approach to Mola Roquerola (see map on page 156). No further details are known.

La Mussara

Mont-ral

Arbolí

Siurana

Montsant

Vilanova de Prades

La Riba

Cogullons

Margalef

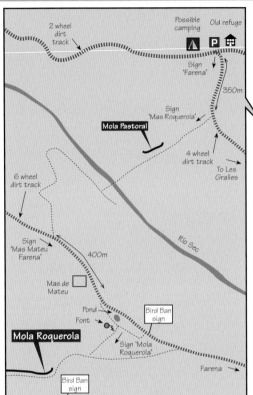

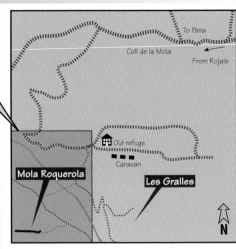

MOLA ROQUEROLA

'High' and 'quality' are the words that best describe the experience to be had at Mola Roquerola. Beautiful bulging white, pocketed waves of bullet limestone perched on a convenient raised ledge system running all the way along the base of the crag. The views are magnificent giving a wide view of the River Brugent and the villages of Farena, Capafonts and Mont-ral.

The routes are predominantly power endurance affairs on sinker-pockets of all dimensions. It is the type of climbing where you have to keep an eye on the footholds as they tend to vanish when you look down. **Hot tip** - don't climb here if you are a bit on the tired side, or fancy an easy day. The climbs are demanding and require a lot of *oomph*. The best routes are in the 6c to 7c range, but a good day can be had for the grade 6 climber. All the routes are well bolted and have lower-offs. This is a sunny crag, but exposed to the elements.

 ## ACCESS

There is a ban on climbing because of nesting Eagles. NO CLIMBING from 1st January to 1st July.

APPROACH - Parking to Crag

The approach is from the parking at the refuge at Cogullons. Follow the approach maps and description carefully or you may not find the crag at all, as a number of people we've met found out. You literally won't see the crag until you are there. Many of the dirt tracks marked as okay to drive in the Spanish guide book and maps are not for two-wheel-drive vehicles (hired or not). As a comparison, the drive to the refuge is a motorway compared to these other tracks.
From the parking area below the refuge, walk south along the 4-wheel dirt track past a signpost to 'Farena'. After 350m you come to another signpost. Go right towards 'Mas Roquerola' along a footpath. The path descends gradually into a wooded area and passes a small sandstone conglomerate crag on the right. Ignore this and begin descending more steeply until you come to a stream. Cross the stream and turn right, heading up stream. The path bends sharply to the left. Follow it uphill until you come to another sign. Take the direction to 'Mas Mateu, Farena' which leads to a 4-wheel dirt track after a short distance. Turn left and head downhill for 400m passing the derelict building of Mas Mateu on your right. You then come to a cleared area on the left. Directly opposite, and hidden in the trees, is the footpath you need to take, marked by a yellow and white painted stone. Head into the under-growth as it bears left and passes a small pond on the left. You will see another sign, next to which is a font (drinkable). Go right following the direction to 'Mola Roquerola'. The path wanders about through the woods until it comes to a T-junction with another footpath. Turn right here and walk uphill following the path which pops you out at a 'Bird Ban' sign and the start of the crag.

Emma Medara through
The Door (7b) Mola Roquerola.
Page 159.
Photo: Highroglyphics

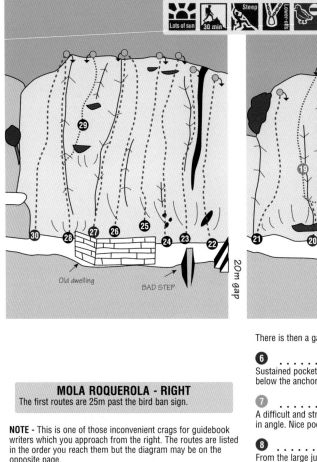

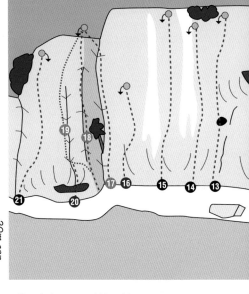

There is then a gap of 10m without any routes.

6 . . . . 🔲 **6b**
Sustained pocket-pulling leads up the wall to easier ground just below the anchors.

7 . . . . 🔲 **6a+**
A difficult and strenuous start leads to a good jug at the change in angle. Nice pocketed wall climbing remains.

8 . . . . 🔲 **6b**
From the large jug on route 7, sustained climbing leads left in a magnificent position.

9 Thin crack . . . . 🔲 **?**

Past a blank white wall is a diagonal crack.

10 Hermes trimegisto 🔲 **7a**
A very mean-looking crack which will probably suck you in and have a good go at spitting you right out.

11 Foc entre les cames . . . . 🔲 **?**

12 . . . . 🔲 **?**

13 Roella blanca . . . 🔲 **7c**
A technical and sequential start leads over the bulge and continues up the superb arm-burning leaning white wall. A real cracker.

14 Kin samalé . . . . 🔲 **7c**
Very attractive climbing leading up the ever-impending wall. Tempting.

MOLA ROQUEROLA - RIGHT
The first routes are 25m past the bird ban sign.

NOTE - This is one of those inconvenient crags for guidebook writers which you approach from the right. The routes are listed in the order you reach them but the diagram may be on the opposite page.

1 ? . . . . 🔲 **5+**

2 ? . . . . 🔲 **6a**

3 ? . . . . 🔲 **5+**
Much trickier than you might imagine for the grade. Climb dribbles of conglomerate deposits on pocketed limestone.

4 Estrellita Castro . . . . . . 🔲 **5**
More pockets on fairly steep ground.

5 B-52's . . . . 🔲 **5+**
A short series of pockets to anchors.

La Mussarra
Mont-ral
Arbolí
Siurana
Montsant
Vilanova de Prades
La Riba
Cogullons
Margalef

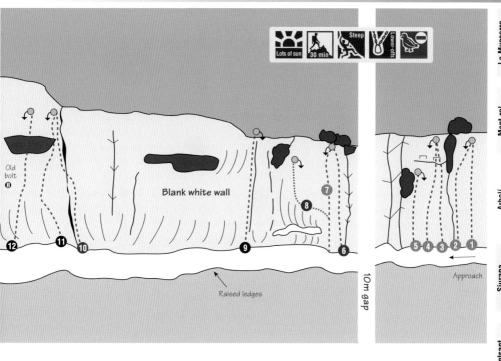

Old bolt ⑧

Blank white wall

⑦

⑧

Raised ledges

10m gap

Approach

La Mussarra

Mont-ral

Arboli

Siurana

Montsant

Vilanova de Prades

La Riba

Cogullons

Margalef

---

⑮ Tónica per tutti . . 🎭📷💧⬜ 7b
A real stunner. See photo inside back cover.

⑯ Situaditis . . . . 📷💧⬜ 6b
Good stonking pockets lead all the way to the anchors. Pity it isn't a wee bit longer.

⑰ . . . . 📷💧⬜ 5+
Clean climbing up the obvious corner.

⑱ Pasión fruite . . . . . 📷💧⬜ 6a+
Very nice climbing taking the prominent rounded arete.

⑲ . . . . 📷💧⬜ 6a
Diverts from *Pasión fruite* into left-hand corner.

⑳ . . . . ⬜ 7a
A brutal and thuggish direct start to route 19.

㉑ . . . . 📷📷⬜ 7a+
A nice looking line which turns out to be very bizarre.

Past 20m of broken ground are some steps with an old ruined dwelling just beyond. **TAKE CARE.** At the top of the steps, there is a gap in the walkway.

㉒ ? . . . . 📷💧📷⬜ 7b

㉓ 'The Door' . . . . . . 📷💧📷⬜ 7b
Photo on page 157.

㉔ ? . . . . 📷💧📷⬜ 7c+

㉕ ? . . . . 📷💧📷⬜ 7c

㉖ La socarrimada . . . . . 📷🤚⬜ 7c+
A steep and powerful start.

㉗ Nefertiti . . . . . . 📷💧🤚⬜ 6c
A tremendous line giving demanding climbing from the start to the very last move. High in the grade. *Photo on page 1.*

㉘ Txop suey de poll . . . . 📷💧📷🔲⬜ 7a+
The big impressive arete left of the prominent groove.

㉙ Curri frai rais viz vegeteibols . . . . . 📷📷🔲⬜ 7b+
Break out right from the arete.

㉚ Penélope . . . . . . 📷📷🔲⬜ 6c
Good climbing on good rock. A touch fluttery if you are not tempted to escape to the left.

La Mussara

Mont-ral

Arbolí

Siurana

Montsant

Vilanova de Prades

La Riba

Cogullons

Margalef

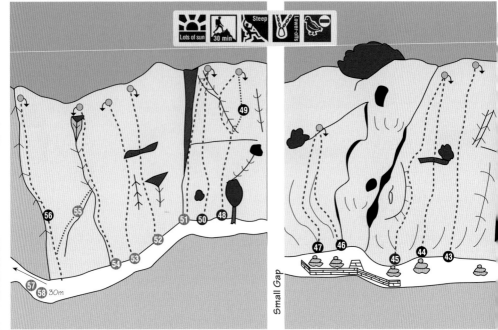

Further along the walkway is another old dwelling.

㉟ Testa di caccio .. 🎰🐚🔪☐ **7c**
Up the black streak.

㊱ Tirant lo blanc ... 🎰🐚🔪☐ **?**

㊲ . . . . ☐ **?**

**㊳ Mirandolina
la pérfida** . . . . 🎰🐚🔪☐ **8b**

㊴ Kabernicolá . . . . 🎰🐚🔪☐ **6a+**
Very interesting climbing leads you away from the ancient fire-place of Mas Roquerola. Moving left, steady climbing breaches the bulges to a good position, then back right across bottom-less grooves to anchors.

㊵ Bolongo hasta la muerte .🐚☐ **7b**

㊶ Familiar monster ... 🐚🔪☐ **7a**
Up the black streak.

㊷ Paella mixta . . . . . . 🐚🔪☐ **7c**

㊸ Desperta ferro . . . . ☐ **?**

㊹ Cagada rock . . . . 🎰🐚☐ **7b**
Strenuous brilliant pocket pulling up the black streak.

MOLA ROQUEROLA - LEFT
The next routes are past a small recess. They are listed in the order you reach them but the diagram may be on the opposite page.

㉛ Umeboshi . . . . 🎰🖾☐ **6c+**

㉜ Ramirurromu . . . . . 🎰🖾☐ **7a**
Technical and thin wall climbing.

㉝ Sisters falo . . . . 🎰🔪☐ **6b+**
Start by bridging up the wide crack leading to the large ledge. Sustained climbing on good pockets and side-pulls up the crack line.

㉞ De negro satén . . 🎰🖾🐚☐ **7b**
Continue moving leftwards from *Sisters falo*, and head up the leaning wall on many small holds.

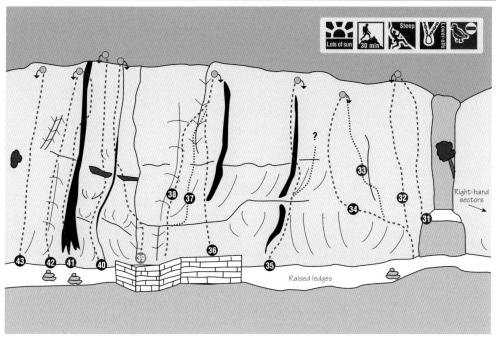

La Mussarra
Mont-ral
Arboli
Siurana
Montsant
Vilanova de Prades
La Riba
Cogullons
Margalef

45 Matute . . . . 🔲🔲⬜ **7a**
Start on the pile of stones, grab the first obvious holds and try and take your feet off the starting blocks. Come back down and have a rethink. Quite a butch pitch. *Photo page 154.*

46 Penitenciàgite . . . . . 🔲🔲⬜ **7c+**
If you think *Bondage* is going to require power, then this one will need mega, mega power.

47 Bondage . . . . 🔲🔲⬜ **7b+**
A short and very bulging route which gives some intense, power-packed climbing.

There is a small gap of broken rock before the next routes.

48 Mandinga bolinga 🔲🔲🔲⬜ **7a**
A difficult route which is hard to read on the crux.

**49 Mandinga
bolinga variant.** . . . . 🔲🔲🔲⬜ **7b**
A harder variant climbing straight up to the anchors at the 4th bolt.

50 La minga dominga . . 🔲🔲🔲⬜ **6c+**
Lots and lots of pockets to choose from, but don't spend too long making a decision. There is a bolt to clip right in the middle of the steep crux sequence.

51 La pinga ferminga . . . . . 🔲⬜ **6a**

Continue past a gully for the next routes.

52 Griego . . . . 🔲🔲⬜ **6a+**
Much trickier and sustained than you might think.

53 Francés . . . . 🔲🔲⬜ **6a+**
A good eliminate starting on pockets and finishing with a reach for the chains.

54 Birmano . . . . 🔲⬜ **6a**
A direct start to *Thailandés*.

55 Thailandés . . . . 🔲⬜ **6a**
Good climbing moving rightwards to the corner.

56 Kamasutra . . . . 🔲🔲⬜ **7b+**
An airy arete gives excellent climbing. Have you got time to admire the view?

The next two routes are to be found 30m left of *Kamasutra* and are poor compared to the other routes.

57 . . . . 🔲⬜ **6a**

58 . . . . 🔲⬜ **6a+**

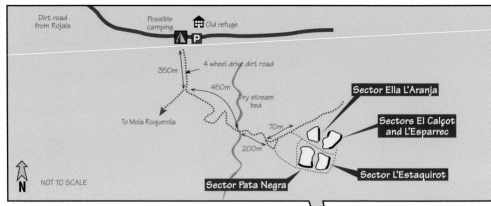

Dirt road from Rojals

Possible camping

Old refuge

350m

4 wheel drive dirt road

450m

Dry stream bed

To Mola Roquerola

70m

200m

Sector Ella L'Aranja

Sectors El Calçot and L'Esparrec

Sector L'Estaquirot

Sector Pata Negra

NOT TO SCALE

N

LES GRALLES

Climbers looking for a good selection of routes in an unusual setting will have a good day wandering amongst the maze of pinnacles and small buttresses of Les Gralles. The various sectors offer varied climbing and, although none of the routes are very long, you will have no problem in logging up some quality climbing time. The crags generally face south but shade can be found if needed.

APPROACH

From the parking area below the refuge, walk south along the 4-wheel dirt track past a signpost to 'Farena'. After 350m you come to another signpost. Go straight on in the direction of Farena. Continue for 450m and cross a dry stream. A further 200m leads to a junction. Go left for 70m and then take a faint path on the right. This leads into a densely vegetated gully between large, isolated cliffs. Continue through the gully to locate the sectors.

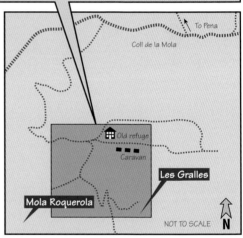

To Pena

Coll de la Mola

Old refuge

Caravan

Les Gralles

Mola Roquerola

NOT TO SCALE

N

SECTOR ELLA L'ARANJA

The best hard routes at Les Gralles are on a wall in the centre of the pinnacles. No significant details or star-ratings are known but they are all good routes

❶ Guaita que fan ara . . . . . 🔶☐ 7a

❷ La trama . . . . 🔶☐ 7c+

❸ La sobredosi . . . . 🔶☐ 7c+

❹ La dosi habitual . . . . . 🔶☐ 7c+

❺ Ella l'aranja . . . . 🔶☐ 7a+

❻ L'escurço negre . . . . . 🔶☐ 7b

❼ Toro sentado . . . . 🔶☐ 7a+

On the opposite wall are two more routes sharing a start.

❽ Gom jabber . . . . 🔶☐ 6b+

❾ Carajillu a'anis . . . . . . 🔶☐ 6a

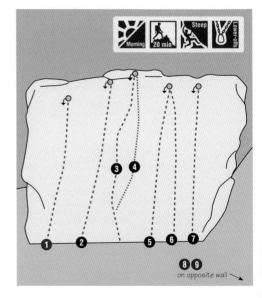

Morning | 20 min | Steep | Lower-offs

8 9
on opposite wall

La Mussarra · Mont-ral · Arbolí · Siurana · Montsant · Vilanova de Prades · La Riba · Cogullons · Margalef

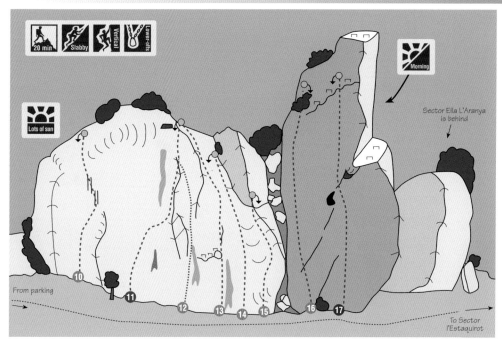

Sector Ella L'Aranya is behind

From parking

To Sector l'Estaquirot

La Mussarra

Mont-ral

Arbolí

Siurana

Montsant

Vilanova de Prades

La Riba

Cogullons

Margalef

SECTOR PATA NEGRA

A fine west-facing sector with enough good routes to fill an afternoon. The rock is good and provides some strong lines. *Pata Negra* itself is an excellent little route.

⊖ - These routes had their bolts removed at the time of writing

⑩ Fulanito de tal **5**
Unusual climbing for this crag - no pockets!
A nice start to your day.

⑪ El Gran Wyoming . . . . . . **4+**
Pleasant climbing on good rock and good holds.

⑫ Txapat per defunció **5**
The bulging prow is the crux of the route, then climb on to the anchor.

⑬ Variant de Txapat . . . **5+**
Nice continuous climbing.

⑭ Tararí que te ví . . . . **5+**
A steep start which soon eases.

⑮ La pila del greix **6a**
You may think this has a steep start but at three bolts long, that's all you get.

⑯ Siames aromatic **6a**
Steep starting moves on lots of pockets.

⑰ Pata Negra **6b**
Quality climbing on quality rock. The trick is to get your hands and feet in the right pockets. Do this and you'll be flowing nicely, don't do it and you'll be back on the ground.

COGULLONS *Les Gralles - Sector l'Estaquirot*

La Mussarra
Mont-ral
Arbolí
Siurana
Montsant
Vilanova de Prades
La Riba
Cogullons
Margalef

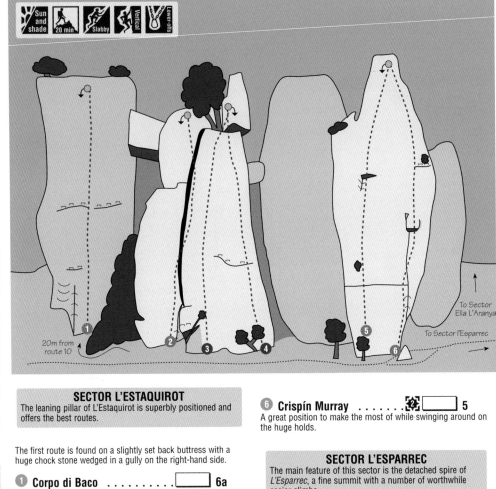

20m from route 10

To Sector Ella L'Aranya

To Sector l'Esparrec

SECTOR L'ESTAQUIROT
The leaning pillar of L'Estaquirot is superbly positioned and offers the best routes.

The first route is found on a slightly set back buttress with a huge chock stone wedged in a gully on the right-hand side.

❶ Corpo di Baco 6a
After the vegetated start, climb straight up the centre of the buttress.

The next routes are found 20m down and rightwards.

❷ Chuper crà 5
An awkward start, then a plod to the top.

❸ Mu bonito 4
Pleasant climbing up the small buttress.

❹ Chupopter .... 4+
Pad up the slab which is split halfway by a ledge.

The next 2 routes are on the front of the pillar which forms an unusual archway from where it leans against the rock behind.

❺ L'Estaquirot .... 5+
Lots of huge holds to grab.

❻ Crispín Murray 5
A great position to make the most of while swinging around on the huge holds.

SECTOR L'ESPARREC
The main feature of this sector is the detached spire of *L'Esparrec*, a fine summit with a number of worthwhile easier climbs.

❼ Pupi chou 6a
A good name but walk on for more tasty fare.

❽ Letania contra el miedo .... 7b+
Good rock, short and hard.

❾ El maleante .... 7a+
A bit gloomy.

❿ ? 6a
Very pleasant and continuous climbing with good positions. Go right to lower-off.

⓫ ? 6a
Great exposure. Go right to lower-off.

COGULLONS *Les Gralles - Sectors L'Esparrec and El Calçot*

La Mussarra

Mont-ral

Arbolí

Siurana

Montsant

Vilanova de Prades

La Riba

Cogullons

Margalet

⑫ Normal de l'Esparrec . . . 🔲 5+
The obvious groove on this pillar offers some very nice climbing.

⑬ Billi Vivillo . . . . . . 🔲 6a+
The difficulties are low down.

⑭ L'Esparracada . . . 🔲 6b+
Excellent starting pockets. The distinct crux moves higher up will have you thinking for a few seconds - some sharp edges on a smooth leaning wall. The shorter you are the more time you will need to think.

⑮ Rampampimfla . . 🔲 6b+
The curving groove has good rock and very good climbing. It is well worth seeking out but is not a good warm-up.

SECTOR EL CALÇOT
A fine little sector giving a guaranteed workout for your fingers. The rock is excellent and, although the routes are short, there are enough of them to fill a morning.

⊖ - These routes had their bolts removed at the time of writing

⑯ Oh noi. . . . . 🔲 6c
Excellent and sustained climbing up a steep shallow corner leads to a point where you may find yourself uttering the route name.

⑰ Bocabadat variant . . . . 🔲 7a+
Slightly harder moves at the bulge.

⑱ Bocabadat . . . . 🔲 7a
Pocket pulling leads to steep moves through the bulge and a good hold. More good climbing takes you to the anchors.

⑲ Macrobiotic no estricte 🔲 6c+
The shallow groove has short lived technical difficulties but the moves are hard and the clips tenuous.

⑳ Pim pam . . . . 🔲 5+
Crack lovers will be drawn towards this. Three times longer and it could get classic status.

㉑ De la bagasseta . . . . 🔲 6b+
Probably doesn't get many ascents but at least the rock is good.

㉒ Wolldam . . . . 🔲 7a
Technical face which unfortunately isn't long enough. A cool and shady route.

㉓ El banyut . . . . 🔲 7b+
A short 7b+, therefore bound to be fierce! It breaches the widest part of the overlap.

㉔ Malestruc . . . . 🔲 7a
A well-positioned arete giving technical and intricate climbing on good rock.

㉕ Escurçons dels Cogullons ⊖🔲 6a
The first route on the wall. As with all these routes a variety of pockets leads you to the top.

㉖ Bestia parda . . . . ⊖🔲 6a
A quick pull on good pockets, but with few footholds, gets you to easier climbing and great views.

㉗ La calçotada . . . . ⊖🔲 5+
A touch easier than its neighbours.

㉘ Tomax . . . . ⊖🔲 6a
Another nicely sustained exercise in pocket-picking.

㉙ Denis . . . . ⊖🔲 6a+
The hardest on this wall. A gentle start on good pockets suddenly leaves you stranded as pocket size and holds reduce dramatically. All fingers and thumbs leads you out of trouble to the anchors.

MARGALEF

La Mussarra

Mont-ral

Arboli

Siurana

Montsant

Vilanova de Prades

La Riba

Cogullons

Margalef

The Margalef Valley with Can Llepafils on the right, above El Laboratori. Photo: Alan James

Margalef is a pleasant little area to the west of the other crags covered in this book. The crags line the sides of a secluded river valley with the various walls protruding from the trees and offering extremes of climbing. There are plenty of pleasant slabs, at friendly grades, which is useful since green-spot routes are in short supply on some Daurada crags. The fine crags of Can Llepafils and Can Torxa are the main attractions for most visitors and these two alone will give a great day's climbing with just the odd complaint about the undercut starts. Next to (or directly below) the pleasant slabs are some of the steepest and wildest formations you will find anywhere, many of which are so radical that they are likely to remain projects for many years to come. In fact the immense cave at the far end of the wall known as El Laboratori has the World's most outrageously-placed lower-off on its lip; 25m horizontal roofs on three sides and no visible holds! However, despite all this steep rock, there is not that much to attract the hard climber since few of the walls have been developed.

THE ROUTES

The rock is a conglomerate similar that found at Montsant, but the buttresses are on a much smaller scale. Most of the climbing involves pulling on big pebbles or holes once filled by pebbles. Many of the walls are steeply undercut giving hard starts but above that the rock usually slabs back to either vertical or even slabby on Can Llepafils.

Although there isn't much for the hard climber, those looking for grades up to 7b will find enough to keep them happy, especially if you dot about the various buttresses a bit.

La Mussarra

Mont-ral

Arboli

Siurana

Montsant

Vilanova de Prades

La Riba

Cogullons

Margalef

CONDITIONS

The left-hand side of this valley (looking up) is a complete sun-trap and can be even hotter than many of the other sun-traps in the Costa Daurada since it is also relatively sheltered. This could well be welcome in the winter months when the Daurada can suffer from crisp but cold days. The opposite side of the valley is in the shade for much of the day, unless you get here early, and can be an excellent hot weather alternative, one of the few in the area. Although there are many steep crags here, you will struggle to find much to do if it is raining since the bulging walls will stream with water.

APPROACH

The valley is situated some distance to the west of the other areas covered in this book. The best road to follow is the C242 which goes through Cornudella and Ulldemolins. Head along this, avoiding any turns to the right until you can turn left down a steep winding road to Margalef. Clock the kilometres at the top of the hill and look out for a turning on the left after 6.3k (there may be some recycled bottle bins on the turning). This leads up a wide valley with buttresses on either side. There is a large parking spot at the beginning of the valley which should be used for the shady-side crags. Further up the valley are various small lay-bys which can accommodate a few cars. If these are full then the walk from the larger parking is not too tiring.

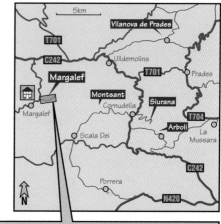

LOCAL FACILITIES

The village of Margalef has a bar and a few small shops. There is also a refuge (enter the village and turn right up a steep hill) however it is rarely open.

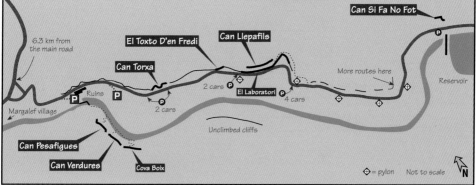

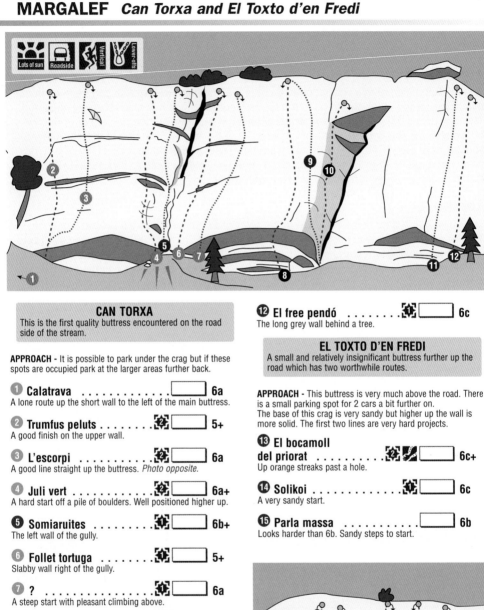

La Mussara
Mont-ral
Arbolí
Siurana
Montsant
Vilanova de Prades
La Riba
Cogullons
Margalef

CAN TORXA

This is the first quality buttress encountered on the road side of the stream.

APPROACH - It is possible to park under the crag but if these spots are occupied park at the larger areas further back.

❶ Calatrava 6a
A lone route up the short wall to the left of the main buttress.

❷ Trumfus peluts . . . . 5+
A good finish on the upper wall.

❸ L'escorpi 6a
A good line straight up the buttress. *Photo opposite.*

❹ Juli vert . . . . 6a+
A hard start off a pile of boulders. Well positioned higher up.

❺ Somiaruites . . . . 6b+
The left wall of the gully.

❻ Follet tortuga . . . . 5+
Slabby wall right of the gully.

❼ ? 6a
A steep start with pleasant climbing above.

❽ Ivan Tres Potes . . 7b
A powerful bulging start leads to a thin upper wall.

❾ Supercalcárea . . . 7a
Trend left towards the arete.

❿ ? . . . . (7a/b)
The steep side wall.

⓫ Freekandó 6c

⓬ El free pendó 6c
The long grey wall behind a tree.

EL TOXTO D'EN FREDI

A small and relatively insignificant buttress further up the road which has two worthwhile routes.

APPROACH - This buttress is very much above the road. There is a small parking spot for 2 cars a bit further on.
The base of this crag is very sandy but higher up the wall is more solid. The first two lines are very hard projects.

⓭ El bocamoll del priorat . . . . 6c+
Up orange streaks past a hole.

⓮ Solikoi 6c
A very sandy start.

⓯ Parla massa 6b
Looks harder than 6b. Sandy steps to start.

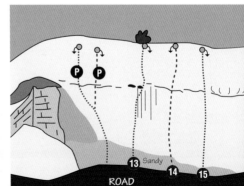

La Mussara

Mont-ral

Arbolí

Siurana

Montsant

Vilanova de Prades

La Riba

Cogullons

Margalef

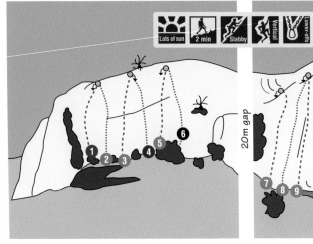

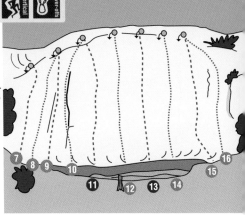

EL LABORATORI

Further up the valley from Can Torxa the lower walls bulge over the road. These walls have plenty of bolt lines on them but most look like either extremely hard routes or very ambitious projects. If you do feel like tackling something a bit harder then the lines to the right of the buttress, before the big cave with the wacky lower-off, look a bit more reasonable.

CAN LLEPAFILS

The most extensive buttress in the valley is perched above the impressive bulging walls of El Laboratori. This has numerous pleasant slab routes especially in the lower grades. It is very exposed to the sun and can be incredibly hot.

APPROACH - Drive down the valley past Can Torxa and continue past El Laboratori and the deep cave on a corner. Park on the next bend. Walk up to the pylon and double back above the big cave to reach the upper tier.

FAR LEFT

The first routes described are on a short wall beyond the main undercut buttress.

① Tampak . . . . **4+**

② A morro **5**

③ Sexi movie **6a**

④ Korroscada . . . . **6b+**

⑤ Eskorbuto **6a**

⑥ Sociedad alcohólica . . . . . . **?**

MAIN

The main buttress has a steeply undercut base giving most of the routes a first-move crux.

⑦ Titacorta . . . . **5+**

⑧ Torrada negra . . . . **5+**

⑨ Bombarda **6a**

⑩ Les mosques
també dormen . . . . **6a+**

After a beefy start, climb the crack.

⑪ Avi que no
has vist livingston **6b**
Another beefy start.

⑫ Smuc . . . . **6a+**
An easier start if you step off the tree stump.

⑬ Besalgato **6b**
Hard start.

⑭ Callaunrato . . . . **6a+**

⑮ Puerto murraco **6a**
Slide around the edge of the low roof.

⑯ Desakato **6a**

La Mussarra

Mont-ral

Arbolí

CAN LLEPAFILS - RIGHT

The centre of Can Llepafils is dominated by an undercut section. To the right the routes are easier but slightly less impressive.

17 Llepafils 5
Left of the scoop.

18 Pampa mik 5
Right of the scoop.

19 Trans . . . . 4+

20 Txak park 4
A high first bolt, but easy climbing.

21 A mi plin 5
Start up a steep bank. Break out left.

22 Pidle soccaret . . . . 5+
Direct verison of the previous route.

23 Miss Tela . . . . 6a+
A thin slab. Start up the steep bank.

24 Tronco quemao 4

25 Katulina . . . . 4+
Left of the big tree.

26 Rosco guarro 5
Right of the big tree.

27 L'homeflor . . . . 5+

28 Cutty Sark 4

29 Raticulin . . . . 5+

30 Tío raro 5

31 Air bamba . . . . 5+

32 Fa fong 5

33 Jungle-jungle 6a

34 Akimatoro . . . . 5+

Siurana

Montsant

Vilanova de Prades

La Riba

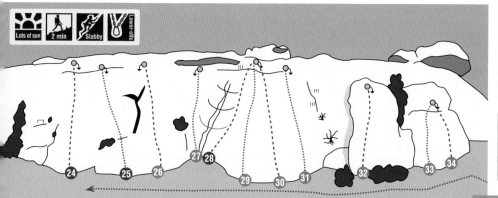

Cogullons

Margalef

La Mussarra

Mont-ral

Arbolí

Siurana

Montsant

Vilanova de Prades

La Riba

Cogullons

Margalef

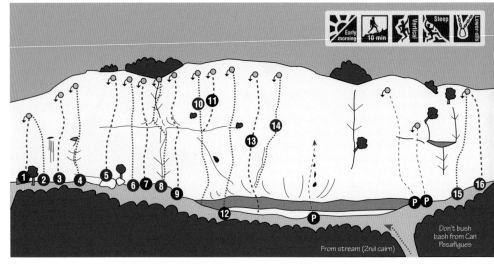

CAN VERDURES

This steep buttress is heavily undercut at the point where the path arrives. The main area of interest is to the left where the upper walls are more accessible.

APPROACH - From the first parking spot, by the ruin and small dam, cross the stream and walk along the right bank for about 300m. The first cairn leads up to Can Pesafigues. The second cairn leads up to Can Verdures. Don't try and get to this buttress from Can Pesafigues without returning to the stream since the bush-bash is awful.

❶ El día de la bestia . . . 🔲 7a+
At the end of the cleared vegetation.

❷ Baginades . . . . 6b+
Left of an orange streak.

❸ Kriliu . . . . 6b+

❹ Murciegalus . . . . 6b+
Up and orange scoop.

❺ Gos roig ros boig . . . 6c
Start from a block.

❻ Samson 7a
Technical moves on the upper wall.

❼ Carn d'olla . . . . 7a+

❽ El senyor de les mosques 6c+
The corner crack and fine upper groove.

❾ O'mar galef 7b
Sustained above the break.

❿ Verdures atómiques 6c
Good climbing on the upper wall.

⓫ Project . . . .

⓬ Bitx 7b
A steep start but the main difficulties lie higher up.

⓭ Ni poc 7b
A steep starting bulge with some painful pockets.

⓮ Estilson 7a
The same steep start is the crux.

The next section has an impressive project. The only other routes are to the right from the approach path.

**⓯ La pernillota
del Passadena** 6b
The wall and slim corner right of the roof.

⓰ La feria choquetin 6b
A thin slab.

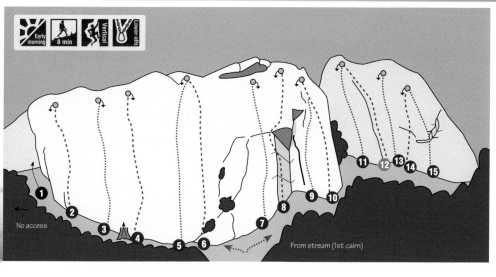

La Mussarra

Mont-ral

Arbolí

Siurana

Montsant

Vilanova de Prades

La Riba

Cogullons

Margalef

CAN PESAFIGUES
The first buttress encountered on the shady side of the stream is heavily vegetated at its base.

APPROACH - From the first parking cross the stream and walk along the bed for about 300m. When you come to the first cairn head up through the bushes.

❶ Project . . . .

❷ Maar Galluf 6c
Start up a white streak.

❸ Bulma . . . . 6b+
Left of the tree.

❹ Sense pi . . . . 6c+
Behind the tree.

❺ Okupa aristo . . . . 6b+
Pocket at the start.

❻ Tasmanian devil 6b

❼ Camborius . . . . 6b+
A slab up the pillar.

❽ El pesafigues 6b
A steep start but a nice upper wall.

❾ Murdol 6b
The right wall and crack in the big red corner.

❿ Escargot boobé . . . . . . 6c+
Tricky start then easier climbing just left of the arete.

The next routes are on the set-back buttress right of the approach path.

⓫ Drac sheran 6a

⓬ La senda de wenda . . . . 5+
A recessed crack.

⓭ Ulls 7a

⓮ El mostre bú . . . . 6c+

⓯ L'estibador 6c

COVA BOIX
The third cairn on the stream-side path leads up to another buttress, via a winding path. This is probably the most impressive buttress in the valley but so far has only two bolt lines. One looks about 7c/8a and was well chalked, the other looks impossible.

La Mussara

Mont-ral

Arbolí

Siurana

Montsant

Vilanova de Prades

La Riba

Cogullons

Margalef

Lots of sun | 2 min | Vertical | Lower-offs

Approach along ledge

6.3 km from the main road

El Toxto D'en Fredi

Can Torxa

Can Llepafils

Can Si Fa No Fot

More routes here

Reservoir

2 cars

El Laboratori

4 cars

Margalef village

Ruins

2 cars

Can Pesafigues

Can Verdures

Cova Boix

Unclimbed cliffs

⊹ = pylon   Not to scale

N

CAN SI FA NO FOT

The final crag described is further up the valley, on the same side as Can Llepafils. The routes here are well-positioned with plenty of exposure.

APPROACH - Drive about 500m beyond the parking space for Can Llepafils. The buttress overlooks the reservoir and is easily reached from the road.

There is another buttress above the lay-by on the corner by a pylon. The routes on this appear to be in the 6c to 8a range.

❶ **Project** . . . .
The steep bulges

❷ **Pilsen** . . . . 　　　 **6c**
The wall left of the open scoop.

❸ **Cop de Cap** . . . . . 　　　 **6c**
The open scoop.

❹ **Figogol** . . . . 　　　 **7a+**
Fine climbing on the wall left of the corner.

❺ **Txana** . . . . 　　　 **6c**
The corner.

❻ **Via del mingo** . . . 　　　 **6c+**
The well-positioned wall on the right. *Photo opposite.*